BY TIM HANSEL
   When I Relax I Feel Guilty
   What Kids Need Most in a Dad
   You Gotta Keep Dancin'
   Holy Sweat

TIM HANSEL

HOLY SWEAT

WORD BOOKS
PUBLISHER
WACO, TEXAS

A DIVISION OF
WORD, INCORPORATED

Unless otherwise noted, all Scripture quotations are from the Revised
Standard Version of the Bible, copyrighted 1946, 1952, 1971 by the Division
of Christian Education of the National Council of Churches of Christ in
the U.S.A., and are used by permission. All rights reserved. Quotations
identified as PHILLIPS are from The New Testament in Modern English
and The New Testament in Modern English, Revised by J. B. Phillips,
published by The Macmillan Company, © 1958, 1960, 1972 by J. B. Phillips.
Those identified as KJV are from the King James Version.

An effort has been made to locate sources and obtain permission where
necessary for the quotations used in this book. In the event of any
unintentional omission, modifications will gladly be incorporated in future
editions.

Permission to quote the poem by Amy Carmichael on page 130 is gratefully
acknowledged and is used by permission of Christian Literature Crusade,
Fort Washington, Penn. 19034. The poems of Norman Habel, "Did You
Ever Doodle, Lord?" and "Some Very Special People" are from Open to
Interrobang by Norman Habel, © copyright 1969 by Fortress Press; used by
permission. The poems of Philip Clarke Brewer, "Paradoxes of a Man of
God" and "Five Loaves and Two Fishes," and Barbara Francken Kelley
© 1983, "Heart of Flesh" and "Burning Bush," are used by permission. "I
Was Hungry" is reprinted from Balcony People, © copyright 1984 by Joyce
Landorf, published by Word Books. "The Towel" by Doug McGlashan is
used by permission of World Vision magazine © copyright 1987. "Joy is the
Flag Flown High," source unknown, is taken from Joy in the New Testament
© copyright 1984 by William G. Morrice and is used by permission of
Wm. B. Eerdmans Publishing Co.

Library of Congress Cataloging-in-Publication Data

Hansel, Tim.
    Holy sweat.
    1. Christian life—1960–   . 2. Success.
I. Title.
BV4501.2.H334   1987   248.4   87-8263
ISBN 0-8499-0627-X

Printed in the United States of America

This edition has been produced for members of Family Bookshelf and is reprinted by arrangement with WORD BOOKS, Waco, Texas.

Contents

Acknowledgments

The future just isn't what it used to be . . .
                                                    —*Anonymous*

It's a delicious thing to write . . .
                                            —*Gustave Flaubert*

I truly enjoy the process of writing. It is one of the greatest
privileges in my life. However, although it is a solitary activity I
never could have written this book without the strong encouragement and support of special friends and co-workers. We are
moving into the most difficult future of all time. It will demand
our very best. *Holy Sweat* was written in the hope of again
discovering "how do we explore and fully utilize the manifold
gifts God has given us?" And what is it all for? What is the
ultimate purpose of this journey called life?

The following people have helped me in countless ways. Not
only have they modeled the message found on these pages, but
they also provided practical ideas and participation. The *Holy
Sweat* film project, on which the book is based, took almost
three-and-a-half years to complete and would not have been
possible without the leadership of Steve Thomsen, Arralee
Hays, D. Paul Thomas, Ken Carpenter, and our incomparable
editor Scott Laster. The *Go For It* footage of our handicapped
climbers was filmed by Jan van den Bjosch and Willem v.
Schaayk. The superb footage from Summit Expedition's *None
Ran Last* film was produced by Jim Vaus and filmed and di-
rected by Steve Craig, who is second to none.

Special thanks is owed to our *Go For It* participants: Julie

Kelly, Bonnie Robertson, Jon Thompson, Peter Jordan, and Janet Fraser—and Summit Expedition's unequaled staff who made this course and film possible and continue to consistently run the finest program in the country. Thanks for your patience with me while I was working on this book. (And Kiwi, we'll run one of these in New Zealand one of these days.)

Erma Barton is the world's greatest administrative assistant. I not only wouldn't have finished this without her; I wouldn't get through a week without her!

Lois Elsensohn, Rick Van der Kam, Jim Wilson, Danielle Lopez, and Scott Harris all worked extra hours to provide the steady leadership of Summit's ministry. It's impossible to thank all the participants, but I'm particularly grateful to Denny Magnuson, Peb Jackson, Christian Okoye, Robert, Chris, and Scotty Noriega, Orv Mestad, Jim Milhon, Shel Jackson, Jerry Waitulavich, David MacPherson, Ken O'Neil, Jerry Heinrich, and Danny Swain who provided the sag support. Bill Snyder deserves a purple heart for all he's done to further God's work through photography and sound.

I don't have enough words to thank Lynda Stephenson for her ingenuity and tenacity. And I am deeply grateful for the wisdom, patience, and expertise of Carey Moore. Likewise, this book would never have reached its full potential without the incredible vision and support of Kip Jordon, Joey Paul, Ernie Owen, Ron Land, and Piers Bateman. And "Bubba"— thanks for being a living example of what this book is all about.

A work that bears a single name should really be inscribed with hundreds of others. To many others whom I have not mentioned here I'm deeply indebted. Obviously, my deepest thanks goes to Pam and Zac and Josh—the family who continues to put up with my late nights and missed basketball games. Zac and Josh—I never realized that being your dad could be so much fun. Pam—I've never loved anyone like I love you. Thanks for making it all worthwhile. Ten years from now I'll love you even more.

Introduction

A little boy asked his mom one day if she knew what Goliath said when David hit him with a stone.

"Why, I didn't know Goliath said anything," his mom replied.

The little boy nodded his head knowingly and said, "Sure he did. When David put that stone in his sling and whipped it around, and let it go and hit ol' Goliath right between the eyes, Goliath said, 'Hmmmm, nothing like that has ever entered my mind before.'"

The aim of this book is to offer you some new ideas, maybe some that have never entered your mind before.

I need to warn you in advance, though, that this is not a cautious book. It's meant to challenge you, to stimulate you, to provoke you to new levels of thinking—and then to action.

Jeremiah 30:2 says, "'Write in a book all the words that I have spoken to you.'"

Over the past two decades, and especially the last seventeen years of my work with Summit Expedition, God has been emphasizing in my life the concepts revealed in this book. I *had* to write it. This book is designed quite literally to change lives. One of its major aims is to remind us constantly that God will supply, but we must apply. I can say that with great certainty, knowing this book has changed at least one life—my own. I've lived this book, and found its truths to work. Its basic theme can be summed up in the title: *Holy Sweat*.

I can hear you now. "How could all that smelly stuff that pours off us when we exert ourselves be—*holy*?!"

It seems like a paradox, doesn't it? Holy—sweat? The two words don't go together. Or do they?

That's just the point. Holy sweat is an "oxymoron"—a descriptive phrase consisting of two apparently opposite words that, when combined, convey a startlingly new and revealing image. Put another way, it's a new concept, fused by means of the juxtaposition of two ideas. It is something that shocks us in a joyful way, and provokes us to a new level of thought. The word *holy* is to remind us of our highest calling. And the word *sweat* is intended to infer the constant change and renewal involved in the process of our getting there. Holy sweat *is* a paradox. *Holy* refers to our common bond, while *sweat* is something we must do on our own.

The Bible is full of many such terms. We are told we must lose our lives in order to find them; we must die in order to live; we must give away in order to have; we must admit we are wrong to be declared right; we are strongest when we are weakest; when we are the least, we are the greatest. Even the incarnation—God becoming man, the Word becoming flesh—is a paradox.

But a paradox is a way of discovering the deepest of truths. The root of the word *paradox* suggests that—*para* and *doxia* mean "alongside glory."

Holy Sweat is such an idea. The image I want it to convey is the active melding of the spiritual and the earthy, the holy and the physical, a profound paradox that lies at the very heart of this life we call Christian. *Holy Sweat* reveals that the holy is here within us, waiting to pour out of us, and that it's much more accessible than we ever would have thought. It's grace with blisters; it's redemption in overdrive.

With just such a startling image, I want to shake your ideas of how you look at the Christian life. I want you to see its paradox, its amazement, and its potential—all within you. The spiritual and the physical can and do meet. We so often make the grave mistake of separating the two, thereby diffusing the power God has planted within us. It is vital for us to remember again that in the opening pages of the Bible, God created

•

"stuff": earth, vegetation, animals, man, woman—not intangibles such as love, virtue, faith, and hope. Those will come soon enough. In the beginning he acknowledged that the physical and the spiritual are not mutually exclusive entities—and this theme remains consistent throughout the Bible.

The Old Testament is crammed with changed lives, with earthy stories, with actual events. It's not a recording of selected concepts and theories. We are not offered abstract and ethereal principles, but real encounters of a living God and his people. The incredible truths of the Bible are revealed to us through genuine life-changing stories, not just through a group of isolated principles to memorize.

Each of us is a one-of-a-kind story as well, through which our Lord continues to reveal himself. I like Elie Wiesel's wonderful statement, "God made man because he loves stories." The word *story* goes back to the Greek word *eidenai*, "to know." Your story is important. How you live it out is vital. And the great mystery of the Bible is that God has said, "Don't let your character be moulded by the desires of your ignorant days, but be holy in every part of your lives, for the one who has called you is himself holy. The scripture says, 'Ye shall be holy, for I am holy'" (1 Peter 1:15, 16 PHILLIPS).

We are called to live a holy life. As far as I know, there are no exceptions. But what does that mean? I believe that holiness must be more than just a concept. Our living is to be holy; our moments of pain, our moments of joy, and our efforts to live life to the fullest can be holy.

As Abraham Heschel once said so beautifully, "Just to be is a blessing. Just to live is holy."

This book is an invitation to a celebration and an adventure. At the core of it is what I call the process of personal peak performance—keys to unlock the holy that is already within you. They are called "keys" rather than principles for a distinct purpose. A key is a relatively small and simple device, but it can be very useful in unlocking something you want. By a simple turning, vast warehouses of resources can be made available to you.

13

They are also called keys because we already carry them with us. My prayer is that one or all of these keys will enable you to release and utilize the incredible potential that God has given you.

I admit that "peak performance" is a somewhat awkward phrase. Our world has coined it to mean an act of accomplishment, a strenuous sort of self-effort mentality we "psych up" for that results in a plaque or a trophy, a higher income or applause, a svelte body or a blue ribbon.

This peak performance concept is not based on accomplishment. This book is not just another "ten easy steps to success." The peak performance concept presented here is a *process*, one that helps form in us a holistic lifestyle based on a deeply spiritual foundation—not toward perfection, but toward *wholeness*. There's a freeing difference.

What, then, is this book? *Holy Sweat* is more a discovery than a set of instructions—an invitation to, and a celebration of, a *hidden adventure*.

Holy Sweat is about servant leadership, about wholeness, about the excitement of unfolding revelation, *about the passion to become the best that you can be—and then to give it all away.* . . .

. . . and at the center of it all, it's about joy.

If you are wondering: "How do I do this?" that is perhaps the wrong question. Instead, I hope we will ask, "How can I *be* this? How do I become who I already am deep inside?"

There are all sorts and varieties of Good News/Bad News jokes. One of my favorites is about the man who goes to see his doctor. The doctor says, "There's some good news and there's some bad news."

The patient says, "Well, doc, give me the good news first."

"The good news," the doctor says, "is that you have twenty-four hours to live."

The patient gasps, "If that's the good news, what is the bad news?"

"Well, the bad news," the doctor continues, "is that I couldn't reach you by phone yesterday."

I accept the estimate of the theoreticians that the average person accomplishes only 10 percent of his or her potential. Author John Powell insightfully explains that amazing fact to help us realize that the average person sees only 10 percent of the beauty in the world around him or her and tastes only a tenth of the *deliciousness* of being alive. "[H]is heart is only 10 percent alive with love and his mind embraces only a small part of the thoughts, reflections, and understanding of which he is capable."

Is that bad news or good news? Well, the bad news is that many people will miss life at its fullest because of mere lack of information or motivation. But the good news is that the best season of your life can be ahead of you no matter what your age or circumstances—if you choose to make it so—because 90 percent of your potential is not only untapped and unused, but also *undiscovered*. That's not just good news, it's incredible news! And unlike the doctor's patient, it's never too late to tap into it.

The Holy Sweat peak performance keys are designed with this in mind. But they are full of surprise. How many peak performance concepts end with giving it all away?

But I'm getting ahead of myself.

You will see. This is an unusual book. And we're called to be unusual people. Perhaps this is not a book of "how to" as much as it is "why not?" Here and now. We need to know the power of Christ within us and tap into that power.

The very first Bible verse I learned was from 2 Corinthians 13:3 (PHILLIPS): "The Christ you have to deal with is not a weak person outside you, but a tremendous power inside you." As the poet Wendell Berry says, we are called to continually "practice resurrection."

Perhaps it is said best by Paul himself in a passage I believe to be one of the scriptural platforms for this book, Ephesians 3:14-21. In the J. B. Phillips translation, it begins under the appropriate heading of "I pray that you may know God's power in practice":

As I think of this great plan, I fall on my knees before the Father . . . and I pray that out of the glorious riches of his resources he will enable you to know the strength of the Spirit's inner-reinforcement—that Christ may *actually* live in your hearts by your faith. And I pray that you, rooted and founded in love yourselves may be able to grasp (with all Christians) how wide and deep and high is the love of Christ—and to know for yourselves that love so far above our understanding. *So will you be filled through all your being with God himself.*

Now to him, who by his power within us is able to do infinitely more than we ever dare to ask or imagine—to him be the glory in the Church and in Christ Jesus for ever and ever, amen. (Italics mine)

That is our goal. And what a goal!

There *is* a danger here, however.

To undertake this process of personal peak performance without understanding *why* we want to live this lifestyle, and *how* to live it, could easily cause many of us to lapse into the traditional ideas of peak performance.

The ropes we use in our Summit Expedition wilderness courses are made of three separate strands woven into one line that can hold over five thousand pounds. One of these ropes is only about as thick as a person's index finger. By itself, one of these strands would be unsafe. But together they're almost indestructible. We trust our lives to these ropes.

Just as it's critical for a climber to have all three strands of his or her rope in good condition, so it is with these ideas. It is critical that you not limit yourself to just knowing *what* a peak performer does, but that you also continually keep in mind *why* a person should do it, and then *how* to make that peak performance a lifestyle of servant leadership—as God planned it all along. All three strands are needed to make us strong. So that's how *Holy Sweat* is structured. First, I explain the *why* of this new lifestyle, then the *what*, and finally, the *how*.

As you read, you may agree or disagree with my ideas. Either way, I'm satisfied. Because either way, you're thinking.

Do you remember the Owl, in *Alice's Adventures in Wonderland*? Alice sought out the Owl because she had heard that he had The Answer. When she found him, she said, "It is said that you alone have the Answer."

The Owl replied, "My friend, as much as is said of me is true." So she asked the Owl her question.

And he answered carefully, "You must find out for yourself."

Alice said angrily, "Did I need the Owl to tell me I must think for myself?"

"But, my friend," the Owl replied. "*That* is the Answer."

I hope as you discover what is inside the covers of this book, you'll be inspired to do some heavy thinking of your own. That's always the answer. Perhaps you'll even invent some of your own keys to add to these. I hope you do. These are just what have worked for me. I've struggled through each of these stages in order to discover the path to wholeness. Through detours and dead ends, cul-de-sacs and crooked ramblings, I've wrestled to make these all a daily, exciting part of my existence. I pray that this is what these ideas will do for you, too. These pages are not intended to be "answers," but windows—and windows are for seeing *through*.

PART ONE

AN ADVENTURE LIKE NO OTHER

The "Why" of Holy Sweat

1
Missing the Adventure

The trouble oftentimes with religious people is that they try to be more spiritual than God himself.

—*Frederick Buechner*

Living the good life is frequently dull, flat and commonplace. Our greatest need is to make life fiery, creative, and capable of spiritual struggle.

—*Nikolai Berdyaev*

In the midst of a generation screaming for answers, Christians are stuttering.

—*Howard Hendricks*

Are you tired of just sitting home every weekend and watching your lawn die? Is your idea of adventure limited to watching the late-night TV special? Or finding a deodorant that lasts twelve hours? Has your spiritual life grown sluggish? Are you becoming more a spectator than a participant in life?

If any of these sound all too familiar, then evaluate yourself by honestly answering the following questions yes or no:

_____ Do you spend most of your Christian life sitting stiffly and quietly in a thing called a p-e-e-e-w?

_____ Have you ever pushed any area of your life to its limits, only to realize that there was probably more to life than you previously thought?

_____ Can you recall the last time you felt unique, fully alive, reaching for all your potential?

_____ Do you sometimes think of Christianity as a nice but, at times, unrealistic religion?

_____ Is your idea of the good Christian life still limited to getting a gold star for attendance or knowing all the words to a printed prayer?

_____ Is your idea of risk putting a fish symbol on your car?

_____ Is your idea of Christian maturity being on three committees at the same time?

_____ Is your idea of holiness being fastidious about Sundays?

_____ Have you ever felt like you're missing something?

Well, if you answered yes to any of the above, you are. You're missing an adventure like no other.

An Adventure Like No Other

What do we mean by adventure? You can answer that question yourself by answering another set of questions:

_____ Have you ever been somewhat bored by it all?

_____ Have you ever felt you're just going through the motions?

_____ Have you ever asked yourself whether or not all your Christian activity is really the same as experiencing the fullness of Christ?

_____ Do you ever find yourself being more concerned about your Christian reputation than the needs of the world?

_____ Have you ever done something so radical for Christ's sake that it got you into trouble?

_____ Have you ever risked it all and lost—and still thought it worth it because it brought you into a deeper relationship with the living God?

_____ Do you really feel like you can "do all things through Christ who strengthens" you? Or are those just nice words to memorize?

_____ Is your faith a dull habit or an acute fever?

Webster's Dictionary defines adventure as "moving into the unknown, an exciting enterprise, a bold undertaking with an uncertain outcome, a remarkable occurrence in one's personal history." Amazingly enough, the word comes from a Latin root which means "to arrive."

Anonymous, quite possibly the most prolific poet and writer of all time, once said, "For life is a mystery to be lived out rather than a problem to be solved." Life is special. It is the very crucible which God has given us to discover, know, and share his son. "The truth is," said Anatole France, "that life is delicious, horrible, charming, sweet, bitter—and that is everything." Many miss this wonder, this fullness, this joy—primarily because they miss the adventure.

From the cradle we understand our need for adventure, even though it is easily lost as we grow older. Most of us experience this need as teenagers whether or not we know it by name. Young people need large doses of adventure in order to change, discover, and grow. If they aren't sufficiently challenged by real-life adventures, they will seek and find fictitious adventures of significantly less value. I'm not at all surprised when I see youth explore drugs, sex, or delinquent behavior. I don't condone it; I'm simply not surprised. Such young people are often seeking their idea of newness and adventure. It is their means of breaking what Paul Tournier, in *The Adventure of Living*, calls "the deadly monotony of a society which to them has become over organized, fossilized and impotent."

I am surprised, though, that Christians who claim the wild message of Jesus Christ aren't out on the edge of adventure more often. I have seen all too frequently young and old alike withdraw beneath the shields of niceness, apathy, and boredom in order to avoid the high cost of loving and serving Christ. The pew has gotten too comfortable, and we are suffering immensely from a paucity of real adventure.

This is one of the prime reasons why a few of us joined together in 1970 to form an unusual enterprise called Summit Expedition. The statement of purpose for this wilderness/ adventure program is that it be "*a process of training people in skills, values, competencies and attitudes to be able to serve Jesus Christ in any environment without perception of limit. "*

Since our beginning, we have had almost ten thousand participants, ranging in age from six to seventy. They have experienced a quality of adventure that has encouraged them to discover not only who they are at deeper levels, but who God is at previously unknown levels of experience.

We have often struggled financially to keep the doors to our ministry open and alive, but it has been more than worth it. Programs ranging from a few days in length to over three weeks have been attended by high school and college students, juvenile delinquents, married couples, dads and their children, leaders seeking more skills, the handicapped, executives, and even members of the United Nations.

Summit's programs invite participants to stretch their horizons of commitment as well as their stamina and skill. One reason why the mountains are so ideal for such stretching is that they are removed away from our everyday lives where we depend on cars, cosmetics, and credit cards. We have become a society more concerned with how we look than how we "see." We don't realize how we atrophy—mentally, spiritually, and physically—in our noisy, cluttered world. But we *can* break away from that sort of existence. A new adventure explodes into being anywhere and anytime a person listens to God and faithfully obeys him.

That is the adventure like no other. It's a surprise-filled journey toward deeply knowing ourselves and the One who made us. Bearing the imprint of Christ as we do and knowing the security that he alone can give, I am surprised that Christians aren't the greatest adventurers on the face of the earth.

Philip Brewer is a man with a remarkable gift for words. He recently gave me this poem to remind me that God simply asks us to give what little we have. Only then can he do what only he can do. This incredible journey begins with who and where we are.

Five Loaves and Two Fishes

God uses
  what you have
  to fill a need which
you never could have filled.

God uses
  where you are
  to take you where
you never could have gone.

God uses
  what you can do
  to accomplish what
you never could have done.

God uses
  who you are
  to let you become who
you never could have been.
     —Philip Clarke Brewer

2
Turning Our Theology into Biography

The Word became flesh—and then through theologians it
became words again.

—Karl Barth

He is asking us to be the chief bearers of His likeness in the
world. As spirit He remains invisible on this planet. He relies
upon us to give flesh to that spirit, to bear the very image of
God.

—Paul Brand

Do you know why most of us miss the adventure? It's because
we've never learned to plug our theology into our biography.

One night on the "Merv Griffin Show," I saw Merv interview some body builders. Merv was standing there, looking at
these guys who had muscles on their muscles, and he asked a
poignant question: "What do you use all these muscles for?"

One guy answered by flexing his muscles in one of those
body-building poses.

"No, you don't understand me," Merv said. "What do you
use all those muscles for?"

The guy said, "I'll show you." And he flexed again, posing in
another way.

"No. No. You still don't understand my question. Read my lips. What do you *use* them for."

And the guy posed again.

The tragedy is, I know some Christians like that. Don't you? They attend church; they go to seminars, conferences, and Bible studies. They keep building up their spiritual muscles, but they don't use them for the reason they were created. They've got muscles packed with knowledge and piety, but their essential purpose and power go unused. So they end up with all this power for show, just to look good, not for action. Sometimes they aren't really aware of it. It can happen to any of us. Sometimes it's so subtle.

The root meaning of *story* is "to know," and knowing in the biblical sense is a very intimate thing. It implies to actually *experience*. It is not just head knowledge, cerebral assent, or muscular posing. John 8:32 says, "You shall *know* the truth and the truth shall make you free." You participate, you experience life, and make it "biographical." So, your theology becomes your biography.

Translating our theology into biography is merely meshing our beliefs into everyday reality. It's that simple, and that profound. It's simple, but that's not to be confused with "easy." It is far from that. In fact, it is perhaps one of life's greatest challenges. God wants to have an unblinking reflection in what we call ordinary. If God speaks to us anywhere, it is in our daily lives. I believe it is more important to *live* one word of Scripture than it is to memorize volumes. And living that one word will be a breakthrough to a whole new dimension of this life we call Christian. It will be a window through which you will see and experience greater fullness in Christ. Helen Keller was struck deaf, dumb, and mute by a virus at the age of nineteen months. She would have remained forever trapped in her prison of silence had it not been for the heroic efforts of her teacher, Annie Sullivan. The turning point in Helen's life came when Miss Sullivan gave her *one* word—WATER. When Helen discovered that one word, she discovered the world. It was the doorway to her future, and she went on to become one of the great human beings on this planet. My hope is that somewhere on these pages, you will discover that "one word" that will irrevocably change your future.

Barth's classic comment that the Word became flesh and through theologians it became words again is all too true.

Are you like me sometimes? Does your Christianity become more rhetoric than anything else? I like to challenge people to "walk their talk"—but find that sometimes I fall into the trap of "promenading my loquacity."

The Incarnation Principle

I was on a plane one afternoon and happened to be reading the New Testament when the lady beside me glanced over and said, "Excuse me, Sir, are you a Christian?"

I said, "Yes, Ma'm, right down to my toes, right down to the marrow of my bones."

She looked at me strangely, and said, "That's an interesting way to put it. What do you mean?"

And we had an intriguing conversation about the "incarnation principle"—about the melding of the spiritual and the physical, about the fact that Christianity is not just a spiritual commitment, but a total commitment. Many of us have never let what we know in our heads seep down into our feet and hands, and the marrow of our bones. We've got this *powerful* faith, but we live as if we don't know what to do with it. I'm reminded of St. Paul's words in 1 Thessalonians 1:2-5 (PHILLIPS): "We are always thankful to God as we pray for you all, for we never forget that your faith has meant solid achievement, your love has meant hard work, and the hope that you have in our Lord Jesus Christ means *sheer dogged endurance* in the life that you live before God, the Father of us all.

"We know, brothers, that God not only loves you but has selected you for a *special purpose*. For we remember how our gospel came to you not as mere words, but as a message with *power* behind it—the convincing power of the Holy Spirit."

More than not, we fail to experience the incarnation principle, not so much because we're unmotivated as it is we're uneducated. Many of us have never fully realized that an adventure awaits us out there. We don't know that the lifestyle we're called to live is radically different from the soft, comfortable, tidy one we see all around us. Why? Sometimes it's because we are thinking "spiritual" rather than total. God's greatest desire is to make us whole, complete in him. It's amazing to realize that every time Christ healed someone, he simply made them whole. It's also important to note that he did each one uniquely. He will make each of us whole in a unique way.

Christians are famous for separating the sacred and the secular. But I don't see God drawing those same kinds of lines. In fact, the only real difference between the sacred and the secular is that the secular doesn't know it's sacred yet.

Our theology must become biography, not only because the world needs it so desperately, but also because that was the supreme example God gave us in Christ. The Incarnation.

"The Word became flesh," John 1:14 says, "and dwelt among us, full of grace and truth." That is what incarnation means. "It is untheological. It is unsophisticated. It is undignified," writer Frederick Buechner has said. "But according to Christianity it is the way things are." The incarnation gives us an ultimate model. If God had wanted to teach us psychology, he'd have sent us a psychologist; if he had wanted to teach us about science, he'd have sent a scientist. But he wanted to teach us about personhood, so he sent a Person, the Word made flesh—not only to show us what God is like, but also what life is like.

"To incarnate" means to embody in flesh, to put into or represent in concrete, tangible form. For example, we are called to incarnate God's love—make it real—as well as his forgiveness. Likewise, we're called to embody his peace, and to live out his hope of justice. But the Bible goes even further than that to say that we're called to incarnate his very Presence, as a continuation of the greatest event in human history. When Moses stood at the burning bush he was told to take off his shoes because the ground on which he stood was holy. "The incarnation means that all ground is holy because God not only made it but walked on it, ate and slept, and worked and died on it. If we are saved anywhere," Buechner explains, "we are saved here. . . . One of the blunders religious people are particularly fond of making is the attempt to be more spiritual than God Himself."

Christianity celebrates the real, the actual, the practical. "Without a firm rooting in creation," Eugene Peterson says, "religion is always drifting off into some kind of pious sentimentalism or sophisticated intellectualism or snobby elitism. . . . The Word became flesh. Things matter. The physical is holy."

God revealed himself through a lifestyle, becoming flesh, matter, substance, real. Hence, God works in the eternal present, through us here and now. He lives *within us* here and now. God wants to bind us back to himself, an act that will result in the life abundant he promised. When God repeats something in Scripture, I am sure it's to make a point. I understand, for example, that in the book of Ezekiel, over sixty times it says, "I want you to know Me."

Any Old Burning Bush Will Do

God has no more ceased being revelation than he's ceased being love. As Major Ian Thomas has put it, "Any old burning bush will do."*

Our hearts beat excitedly over stories of people like Abraham and Moses, yet we fail to recognize that they were as frail and nervous as we are. We stand in awe of Moses at the burning bush: "Now there is a bush that burns," we say. "I would like to be a bush like that, but I'm just a heap of ashes." And that's as far as we get.

We discuss the phenomenon of what God can do in a life, tell amazing stories about it, praise it—but then resign

---

* I am indebted for this concept to Major Ian Thomas, and I highly recommend his classic book, *The Saving Life of Christ.*

30

ourselves to being nothing more than what we think we are, a mere bystander, resigned to sitting in the balcony among the spectators.

But it is not the *bush* that sustains the flame. It is *God in the bush, and so, any old bush will do!*

The shocking message of the Bible continues to be that God has chosen the least suspecting of all vessels to do his greatest work. What you are at this particular moment in your life is irrelevant—your nationality, your education, your personality, or how you are physically, spiritually, and otherwise. Who you are is likewise irrelevant. What counts most is what and who you are willing to become. See that scruffy-looking bush over there? That bush will do. See this funny-looking bush over here? It will do too.

Thomas writes, "Moses had to discover this and you will too! He had to discover that a fine physique and noble ambitions, royal breeding and Egyptian scholarship could never be a substitute for that for which man was created—God Himself!"

We tragically have thought that becoming a Christian is a matter of conforming to a certain pattern of behavior, a certain image of preconceived holiness. Our problem is that we've continually viewed the incredible power of God from a distance. God called Moses by name—but *when* did he call him? That is the key. Did he call Moses while Moses stood admiring at a distance? No, God didn't reveal himself until Moses "turned aside to see."

Perhaps you're wondering why you've never experienced the passionate Presence of God. It could be because you're standing back, viewing Christianity from a distance. It is quite possible that your life could remain powerless and unused by God simply because you never took the time to understand why God uses men and women for his great purposes. You've never thought about translating your theology into biography.

"All you need is what you have, and what you have is what He is! He does not give you strength, He is your strength!" Thomas states. He does not give you joy, he *is* your joy. "Christ in you—nothing less than that. You cannot have more—and you need not have less."[1] Talk about adventure!

God's truth is written in our blood, our bones, our breath, our eyes, our ears, and every part of our body. Christianity is not just a spiritual commitment but a total commitment of our intellect, our bodies, and our souls. And this is the underlying reason, the *why*, for pursuing our peak performance lifestyle.

Why then aren't we more aware of this idea? Why do we fall into a boring, complacent lifestyle that is only "Christian" around the edges? God has given us astonishing evidence of who he is, countless astonishing stories in Scripture to prove what he can do through us, and he's come to us in astonishing fashion through Christ. He is, in fact, God's "unexpected Word."

Astonish Me!

We need to be unfettered from our stale, sterile images of God. Most of us don't even begin to comprehend God's incredible audacity in Jesus Christ. Becoming aware of who God is begins with wonder.

I'm beginning to believe that "astonishment" is Yahweh's middle name. The Bible is packed with constant surprise, and encounters that almost defy description. There is a stunner on nearly every page. And the more I read it the more "wonderfull" it becomes, and the more I stand aghast at God's obvious desire to touch us and use us. The evidence is there, in our Scriptures—if we see it.

Many of us have one of two basic problems with Scripture reading. One is that many of us are unfamiliar with the Scriptures. We don't know enough of God's promises to claim them, enough of God's character to be like him. The second problem is much more subtle and dangerous—we can become *too* familiar with the Bible's stories and characters so that they no longer astound us. They no longer arouse us.

Just think of them, though:

• In the opening pages of Scripture, amidst the stupendous flourish of creation, we are told that the culmination of all God's artistic ecstasy is that he created man—in his image, no less . . . out of dirt. A moral agent out of mud.

• He chooses a barren, grumpy old couple named Abraham and Sarah to give birth to a nation that would change human history for all time. Can't you see Sarah laughing in her 90-year-old apron?

• Then he decides to save this unique nation from captivity through an unemployed Egyptian-Israelite prince who tends sheep and stutters. He reveals himself to the man through a scrub bush. And later he puts the Red Sea on dry cycle long enough to allow this ungrateful nation to cross.

• He chooses a teenager who doesn't even have his high school diploma yet to nail a nine-foot enemy right between the eyes with a rock. The boy grows up to become "a man after God's own heart"—even though the man pulls off one of the biggest blunders in the Old Testament.

Doesn't all this have a bit of stylistic news to it? If we were hearing these stories for the first time, what would we think? There's nothing predictable about any of this, nothing logical. One of Summit Expedition's exceptional instructors, Rick Vander Kam, was asked not too long ago, "Hey Rick, what are you going to be doing five years from now?"

His answer is worth remembering. He began, "I don't know."

To which his friend remarked, "What's the matter? Don't you have dreams? Don't you have goals? Don't you have plans?"

Rick answered, "Of course I do. I've written down my goals and I've got incredible, specific plans, but I happen to be following Somebody who is *notoriously unpredictable.*"

He's right on the mark. There's nothing predictable in any of this, and countless biblical stories attest to that. The list of the shockers could go on endlessly.

The New Testament opens with the most flabbergasting incident of all time—that same Author of creation decided to reveal himself by being born . . . in a barn . . . to a virgin.

Later he set about astounding those around him:

• He took a trusting kid's leftover lunch and fed enough people to fill the Hollywood Bowl and still had enough left over for each of the disciples to have his own take-home basket. Can you imagine what they were thinking and how these men felt on the way home?

• He outrageously shocked, surprised, and exasperated the religious community of the time, the Pharisees. When they brought him a woman caught in adultery, he wrote something in the dirt and asked the sinless to throw the first stone. When they dared him to break the Sabbath laws, he did so while quoting Scripture.

• He went to parties with people of questionable social standing and morality, and threw "respectable" tradesmen from the temple's steps. He called Herod "that fox," and was himself looked upon as "a wine bibber and a glutton, a friend of outcasts and sinners."

• Rather than sharing the news of who he really was with the proper authorities, he revealed who he really is to a . . . Samaritan . . . woman who had had a handful of husbands and lovers. Doesn't that at least confuse your prayer life?

• He chose the number one persecutor of his followers to become his top evangelist. And then he gave the keys to the kingdom to the disciple who failed him so badly he denied him three times in one night.

Is this what we call commonplace? If this is dull, then what is worthy to be called exciting? There must be something incredibly unexpected and dynamic to this Creator if these stories are as true as we know them to be. Frederick Buechner says:

Those who believe in God can never, in a way, be sure of Him again. Once they have seen Him in a stable, they can never be sure where He will appear or to what lengths He will go, to what ludicrous depths of self-humiliation He will descend in His wild pursuit of man. If holiness and the awful power and majesty of God were present in this least auspicious of all events, this birth of a peasant's child, then there is no place or time so lowly or earthbound but that holiness can be present there too. And this means that we are *never safe, that there is no place that we can hide from God, no place where we are safe from His power to break in two and recreate the human heart because it is just where He seems most helpless that He is most strong, and just where we least expect Him that He comes most fully.*[2] (Italics mine)

Maybe we prefer not to take these stories too seriously, for if we do, we have to admit their meaning is disturbing. The official story is, as Dorothy Sayers has said, that this wasn't just a good man trying to be like God—but he was God himself. And how did we respond? The common people indeed heard him gladly, but our leading authorities in church and state considered that he talked too much and uttered too many disconcerting truths. So we bribed one of his friends to hand him over quietly to the police, and we tried him on a rather vague charge of creating a disturbance and had him publicly flogged and hanged on the gallows, thanking God that we were "rid of the knave."

And the truly sad part is that now we are no longer shocked by this fact of history. We can get more concerned over the death of our pet goldfish than what happened to Christ on Golgotha. The story has become so familiar and commonplace like the other stories in Scripture, that it no longer shocks us, no longer repels, no longer arouses us. At times, it may not even excite us.

Yet the people who crucified Christ never thought Jesus a bore. The fact is they thought he was fiery and dangerous to public safety. It was left up to us through the years to turn this Person "meek and mild," smiling harmlessly from a framed portrait on a wall. Yet he was the farthest thing from a dull man during his time on earth. And since he was God, there can be nothing dull about God, either.

But let me take this one step further, a step that's vitally relevant to this book. Could we then not say that God's nature has something to do with his will for our lives? That is, when we say "God is love" we aren't just referring to some mush of divinity, some ectoplasmic Valentine, but that since he is love he wants us therefore to be loving. When we say that God is just and forgiving, then we are to be just and forgiving in return. Who God is—that is what he wants from us. The way God is—that is the way he wants us to go. The statements of God in the Bible are boomerang-shaped. They come back to us. So if he is by nature astonishing, then he wants us to live a life of wonderment in return. He says, "Astonish *me!*"

Can we astonish God? We may not think we have the qualifications to, but think of Moses, and Peter, and Mary Magdelene and a host of the other biblical characters. None of them was "qualified." Doesn't that give us hope and encouragement that God can use any of us? All of us? God is saying to us, "Don't just exist. Don't just meet my bottom line. Don't just get by. Don't just go through the motions, acting holy, sleepwalking through life."

And yet he's also given us the choice to do just that. We can choose not to be astonished anymore. We have the right to be bored, to miss the adventure. It is our choice.

Yet, thankfully, he keeps offering the adventure to us. He still says, "Astonish me! Let the herd graze where they may, but you be different. Discover my power in you. Live your theology as biography."

The "Fifth Gospel"

Personally, I believe God is waiting and willing to reveal things that will radically change the lives of people. I believe He is eternally waiting and eager to call forth something from you that has never been said or thought of since the beginning of time. You may be the one in your own field or area of interest to find that all the good things haven't been said or done or even thought of.

—Bruce Larson

There are only four Gospels in the Bible: The Gospel according to Matthew, Mark, Luke, and John. These first-century men, though, were not necessarily professional writers. Why and how did they begin writing? What was their experience? Even a superficial reading of the New Testament will soon reveal that each of the Gospels is very different. The writers were simply inspired to express in words what their encounter with Jesus Christ meant to themselves and those around them. They had no idea what impact their writing would have. I don't imagine they thought history would be changed forever when they crafted their sentences. They just wrote of the life-changing Christ they knew. Matthew wrote from a primarily Jewish standpoint, while Luke saw him and his undeniable compassion from a physician's viewpoint. Mark, being younger, wrote of his understanding from a fast-paced, action-packed angle. Some have called it almost a motion picture of the Gospels. And we are all blessed that John wrote vividly from a poetic mind. His writings have given us some of the greatest metaphors of the Bible. Likewise, each of us, because of his or her truly unique encounter with the living Christ would express that experience in different words. And in a very real sense, as Larson said, the good news continues. What is your unique experience? Writing can be a form of visible prayer.

It is an awesome thought that God actually speaks to us through his Word and his Spirit today. If we know that each of us is absolutely unique, then our encounters with God will likewise be unique. No one will ever have the same relationship with God that you do. No one. Each of our lives and words, then, will be, in a metaphorical sense, a "fifth Gospel"—our own biography of Christ, as he reveals himself to us, and as we look for those "burning bush" experiences.

"When you read this," Paul wrote in Ephesians 3:4, "you can perceive my insight into the mystery of Christ." We are, in a sense, walking Gospels as we *re-present* Christ to the world through our "fifth Gospel." And when we consider our own walk as a unique story, we cannot help but take seriously each moment of our astonishing relationship with the God of the Universe, the God of our daily lives.

A dear friend wrote the following words to remind us that God wants and needs to continually "write on our lives" and express himself uniquely through each one of us. I trust they will ignite you as they did me, to live and write and do whatever you do in the pulsebeat of your own experience.

> It's been so long
>> since I've seen a burning bush
>
> Some seasons
>> I see them
>> in every desert wash
> The magnificence,
>> the miracle . . .
>
>> "burning
>> and not being consumed."
>
> Yet who do I fool?
> Moses paid dearly
>> for his burning bush—
>> sweaty desert miles
>> and exhausted, sweaty tears—
> All for the dubious blessing
>> of talking with God.
>
> What claim have I to a burning bush?
>> (or to God?)
>
> I have not yet even learned
>> to remove my shoes!

38

I've learned so much of me.

        Every inch of it has hurt . . .
        to see honestly
            and at length . . .
        because at first
            all I could see
            were the wounds of humanity.

I looked for cool,
        unflawed
            marble
                of deity
            but found only a heart
            of flesh . . .

        But hearts of flesh
            are all that God
                can write on.

Write on me,
        Father,
Write on me.
                —Barbara Francken Kelley

3
The Christian Life
Is Not What It Seems

There he is. In the temple again. Causing trouble. Speaking very differently from other preachers. Speaking with authority about sorrow, anxiety, sickness, and death. Penetrating the dark corners of human existence. Shattering illusion. Make no mistake about it; this is a dangerous man.

—*Martin Bell*

A man was asked to speak to a rather large church congregation. After he strode to the pulpit he said, "There are three points to my sermon." Most people yawned at that point. They'd heard that many times before.

But he went on. "My first point is this. At this time there are approximately 2 billion people starving to death in the world."

The reaction through the congregation was about the same, since they'd heard that sort of statement many times before, too. And then he said, "My second point. . . ."

Everybody sat up. Only ten or fifteen seconds had passed, and he was already on his second point?

He paused, then said, "My second point is that most of you don't give a damn!"

He paused again as gasps and rumblings flowed across the congregation, and then said:

"And my third point is that the real tragedy among Christians today is that many of you are now more concerned that I said 'damn' than you are that I said that 2 billion people are starving to death." Then he sat down.

The whole sermon took less than a minute, but it is in many ways one of the most powerful ones ever given. In no uncertain terms, he was reminding those of us stuck in our pews that we are called not to mere piety but to genuine morality. We are called to action, not to fancy words. We are members of the kingdom of God, not the kingdom of niceness.

The Christian life is *not* what it seems. Oftentimes we can become (sometimes without even being aware of it) committed to our own happy idea about the Christian faith. We become addicted to comfort and convenience, the good life, convinced it is somehow related to the truth of Scripture. Deep down, we want to believe that if we're Christians we should be good people and good things should happen to us.

But that's not what Christ calls us to. The problem with the "success gospel" is that you can't preach it to two-thirds of the world. I am well aware that we don't need more guilt to paralyze us, but all of us could stand a little more honesty and responsibility. In fact, even as I write these words I am also quite aware that I am still much more a part of the problem than of the solution.

The Kingdom of Niceness

I am convinced we can detour God's great work in our lives not just by the bad things we do but sometimes by the good things. As writer William McNamara puts it, "We limit what God can do in our life by doing so many good things, because we think those good things become a substitute for God himself." Our good, as it's been often said, can become the enemy of our best. Our religiosity, our "niceness," can actually get in the way. When we feel the basic purpose of our faith is to be nice and good, we are confusing the *expressions* of the lifestyle with the *purpose* of it.

Some of us really believe that the point of Christianity is to look good and have a good Christian reputation. But the kingdom of God is a *life-changing, life-transforming experience*. It's more than just . . . nice.

41

Jesus, to the contrary, was shocking, astonishing, loving, daring, revolutionary, kind, caring, compassionate . . . but *nice?*

"To have experienced Christ, to have encountered Jesus of Nazareth, to have run headlong into the person of God in the flesh must have been like stepping into the path of a hurricane. No one would do it intentionally."[3]

Yet how many churches could be described as a "*dangerous* place," a place where someone might warn, "If you go there, your life will get changed! You better watch out"? How are our churches usually described? In warm, comfortable terms.

The Bible does not give us much reason to believe that being saved is in any way to be equated with being safe. For instance, we often hear that Daniel's faith got him out of the lions' den, but we forget that it also got him *into* the lions' den. God doesn't promise us safety, but strength. Jesus is the answer, but he's also the question. Statements like "being in the bosom of Abraham"—"the Lord is my light and my salvation; whom shall I fear?"—and all the other ways the Bible expresses our true security don't mean we will never experience troubles or that we should hide from them. "It's a great comfort to know," says Lloyd Ogilvie, "that God's faithful people have always been in trouble. In fact it's the sure sign we're following God, and not men."

A life of faith calls us to gamble our lives on Jesus Christ. I've got a friend who always reminds me that Jesus promises us at least four things—peace, power, purpose . . . and *trouble.* God doesn't promise a carefree life; he promises peace and joy in the midst of the trouble (John 16:33). There is danger in too much security, and he knew it. As one writer prays, "Oh Lord, secure me from security, now and forever."

Sometimes, we are forced into the "niceness" rut, and find it almost impossible to climb out. Even our spiritual leaders have to fight this mentality.

My friend Rev. Vic Pentz explained the problem with a classic illustration. One day he asked our congregation, "Do you realize what it takes to become a pastor today? In order to have the best shot at becoming a minister, you should go to a good school, preferably a Christian one, make good grades, and be a good kid. Then you should go to college, preferably a Christian one, be a model student, stay within the accepted boundaries of behavior, and make excellent grades. Then you must go to seminary, the right sort of seminary, where you have to be a good person, a model student, and stay within the accepted, appropriate boundaries of behavior and belief—if you want to graduate from seminary and get a good position in a nice church. And then, to be accepted as a pastor after you gain that nice position in a nice church, how are you supposed to behave? Proper. Appropriate. Nice. Staying within the accepted boundaries of behavior and belief—the model Christian leading the model Christian life from cradle to pulpit to grave."

Vic paused a moment, and then shaking his head, he said, "No wonder we call churches non-'prophet' organizations!"

My image of Christians as I was growing up was puny to say the least. I vividly remember a picture of Jesus that hung on the wall of the church meeting hall. My first impression of Jesus from that picture was not that great. He just wasn't my type of man: He was dressed in a flowing pinkish-white robe, with an emaciated look on his face like he'd just sucked on a lemon or drank too much prune juice. His ethereal appearance, especially his long, wispy hair, made him look unmasculine and undernourished.

The picture made him look sober and unsubstantial—as if he had been diluted of all his manhood. And he had a halo, which didn't help matters much. I remembered stories about this gentle Jesus, meek and mild, and that picture of him pretty much fit the image. So even though I was surrounded by some wonderful Christian people, I somehow formed a picture of Jesus—and, hence, his followers—as "wimps."

The reason I am a Christian today is not because I heard the gospel, but because I *saw* it. In graduate school at Stanford I encountered a man by the name of Bob Reeverts. I had never met a man quite like him. He had a strength and a joy that I had never experienced before. Here was a 6'4" man, exuberant with a boundless energy which was outrageously contagious. Without ever intending it, he aroused in me a tremendous curiosity. His life was so different and distinct that it was as if someone had put salt on my lips. I thirsted to know what made this man the way he was. The second time I met him only made matters worse. I couldn't figure out what made him tick. It wasn't what he said that made an impression on me as much as it was *who* he was. On my third encounter with him, I finally couldn't stand it any more. I went up to him and asked him why he was so different. His answer was forthright and succinct: It was Jesus Christ.

I felt like someone had thrown a monkey wrench into my computer. That answer didn't fit any of the puny "twinkie" images I had of what a Christian was. Bob worked with Young Life, an organization dedicated to working with young people around the world for Christ. They were undoubtedly the craziest and most creative group of people I had ever seen. I was thoroughly confused. These wonderful, fun people were seriously denting my somber, subdued, soft-spoken image of Christians. My cardboard image of Jesus was also taking a beating because of the truth made visible by this man and his friends.

Clarence Jordan, author and founder of Koinonia Farm, said,

It is difficult to be indifferent to a wide-awake Christian, a real live person of God. It is even more difficult to be indifferent to a whole body of Christians like this. You can hate them or you can love them, but one thing is certain. You can't ignore them. There is something about them that won't let you. It isn't so much what they say or what they do. The thing that seems to haunt you is what they are. You can't put them out of your mind any more than you can shake off your shadow. They confront you with an entirely different way of life—a new way of thinking, a changed set of values, a higher standard of living.

In short, they face you with the kingdom of God. There is no washing of hands. These people must be crowned or crucified, for they are either mighty right or mighty wrong.

Even though he never knew it, Bob Reeverts made an indelible and eternal impact on my life. It was the beginning of the most important change in my life.

An ancient proverb says:

I heard and I forgot; I saw and I remembered; I did and I understood.

It was in seeing the gospel full of life, experiencing it firsthand, that forced me to begin asking some serious questions.

In my life, there have been no sudden flashes, no thunder and lightning bolts or raising of hands. Some people can point to the time and place they became a Christian with exact certitude: "It was 8:32 P.M. on November the 4th, 1972," they might say, "and I was attending a revival meeting . . . or a Bible study . . . or a church service, when I came to accept Jesus as Lord and Savior." But I had no such Damascus-road experience. The "Hound of Heaven" simply persisted and insisted, sticking with me until I could no longer ignore him. Bob and the Young Life staff were more than "nice"; they were dynamic—authentic—committed to the real Jesus Christ. And my life has been drastically, wonderfully changed because they chose to be members in good standing of the kingdom of God instead of the kingdom of niceness.

Reckless Christianity

Youth speaker and author Dawson McAllister says that the hardest kids to reach with the "true-truth" of the gospel are the "lifers." A lifer, according to Dawson, is somebody who's been raised in the church and has heard the gospel so many times that it has no power any more. Adult "lifers" may be even more deaf to the shocking message of the gospel.

A theologian once said that perhaps the best thing that could happen to all Christians would be for all of us, every three years, to forget everything we've ever known about Jesus—and start all over again.

We need to let go into a "reckless abandonment" of the spirit. To do so is actually a form of worship. As I understand it, one of the root words for worship implies "reckless abandonment, or "care-lessness," worship with a sense of totality and *freedom.* We're called to such freedom.

On every page of his devotional classic, *My Utmost for His Highest,* Oswald Chambers challenges you to make your life match your highest calling. Although conservative in his theology and robustly biblical, he surprisingly uses the phrase "reckless abandonment" quite often to refer to the kind of faith we're called to:

> Faith is the heroic effort of your life. You fling yourself in reckless confidence on God. God has ventured all in Jesus Christ to save us. Now He wants us to venture our all in abandoned confidence in Him. . . . The real meaning of eternal life is a life that can face anything it has to face without wavering. . . . Again and again, you will get up to what Jesus Christ wants, and every time, you will turn back when it comes to that point, until you abandon resolutely. . . . Jesus Christ demands that you risk everything you hold by common sense—and leap into what He says. . . . Christ demands of the man who trusts Him the same reckless spirit. . . . that is daring enough to step out of the crowd and bank his faith on the character of God.[4]

Every once in a while I believe we need to stop and check our spiritual pulse. Are we compassionately involved, stretching ourselves past those boundaries of niceness and piety? There's only one good reason we could live life like that— because God is so trustworthy.

One day, while my son Zac and I were out in the country, climbing around in some cliffs, I heard a voice from above me yell, "Hey Dad! Catch me!" I turned around to see Zac joyfully jumping off a rock straight at me. He had jumped and *then* yelled "Hey Dad!" I became an instant circus act, catching him. We both fell to the ground. For a moment after I caught him I could hardly talk. When I found my voice again I gasped in exasperation: "Zac! Can you give me *one* good reason why you did that???"

He responded with remarkable calmness: "Sure . . . *because you're my Dad.*" His whole assurance was based in the fact that his father was trustworthy. He could live life to the hilt because I could be trusted. Isn't this even more true for a Christian?

Christians can be the freest and most exciting people in the world because they have such a trustworthy and faithful Father. Yet we're so conservative. I heard a definition of a conservative the other day: "A conservative is one who sits and thinks. Mainly sits."

Why should we jump into any of the ideas in this book? Because God is so incredibly faithful. If I'm trustworthy enough that my son can live life with reckless abandonment, then God is infinitely more trustworthy and we can embrace our freedom, and live like Jesus did.

Such freedom, though, is scary, and frequently unpredictable. Our human nature is to lean more toward security, no matter how trustworthy we know God to be. If only we could know what will happen . . . if only we knew how things were going to turn out. But what has Jesus always answered those who asked for a peek into the future?

Another of Summit Expedition's committed instructors, Jim Ungaro, recently asked God for a three-year plan for his life. "Just a little blueprint, Lord," he asked. "What is life going to be like? I just want to be a good steward of my time and talents."

Later, I asked him, "Well, did he give you an answer?"

Jim said, "I got an answer, all right. He said simply and firmly: '*Follow me.*'"

The Boring Christian Life

You can live on bland food so as to avoid an ulcer; drink no tea or coffee or other stimulants, in the name of health; go to bed early and stay away from night life; avoid all controversial subjects so as never to give offense; mind your own business and avoid involvement in other people's problems; spend money only on necessities and save all you can. You can still break your neck in the bathtub, and it will serve you right.

—Eileen Guder, *God, But I'm Bored*

I want to simply ask you one question:
Is your Christian life sometimes boring?
If the answer is yes (and if we are honest, most of us have to confess that to be true sometimes), then I've got a suggestion. Move it to the edge.
Look at this drawing below:

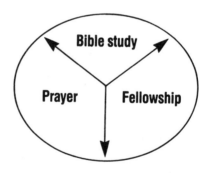

These are considered the fundamental areas of Christian growth. Most of us at some time or another end up getting bored with one or all three. "Oh," we say, "my fellowship would be okay if there were only more neat people like me. And my prayer life would be better if I could just find time alone, or read a better book on prayer."
Ever have that feeling? I have.

How do you find relief from that boredom? I've found one way that I guarantee will work. You simply move your life over to the edge of the circle. When you begin to hang off the edge of your preconceived limits, hanging on by your toenails, your prayer life will come alive, your Bible study will sing, and your fellowship will blossom.

When I was working in a halfway house on New York's Lower East Side, I slept in the bunk below a guy named "Hatchetman." He was 6'5", with arms the size of my legs. One day I asked Bo Nixon, the head of our project, where the guy got his nickname.

"Oh," Bo said, "that's his favorite weapon."

I remember wishing I hadn't asked. But I guarantee it had a great impact on my Christian growth. Suddenly, my prayer life was great, my Bible study increased tremendously, and my need for fellowship went up drastically.

Likewise, when we take people rappelling on our Summit Expedition courses, we find they are anything but apathetic. We have a couple of rappels that would probably make your navel pucker. But afterward, these climbers always talk about the thrill, the joy, of pushing to the edge, trusting those ropes, and feeling an indelible aliveness. It's the same way when we're living out there on the edge of our preconceived notions of what the Christian life is supposed to be. We feel alive, we feel close to God, and we experience tremendous joy.

That sort of experience won't happen if we don't move out onto the edge of our preconceived limits. When we give in to those preconceived limits, however we've acquired them, (1) we never know who we really are and who we can be; (2) we never know what life can be and what its possibilities are; and (3) we never know what God can really do in and through our lives.

In 2 Corinthians 1, Paul writes that when he came to the end of his tether, he really discovered what God could do. When I came to the end of my tether, I found the same thing true. When I was forced to have a radical dependence on God,

I saw him working in exciting ways. On this principle we've based Summit Expedition. We go to the wilderness because the wilderness in Scripture has always been a place for radical dependence on God. In fact, it was consistently God's great place of preparation and training. The Israelites during the Exodus were led only one day at a time. They never had enough manna for more than one day. And when they tried to store up some, it turned rotten before the next day.

It's like Oswald Chambers has said, God is present *now*, "dancing on the chaos of my life." We feel him there when we risk. We see what God can do when we risk being involved in the needs of the world, when we risk pushing through our preconceived limits. Look at the lives of the people of history you admire. They were all living out there on the edge.

Contrary to what you may have heard, we are not called to live *for* Christ. We're called to live *in* Christ. The Gospel of John is constantly talking about "dwelling." I once heard a pastor say that John used the phrase "believe in me" 198 times in his writings. It was his most dominant theme. The Christian life is not just one of imitation—but *habitation*. He's already within us. The power is there. The choice is ours to release it.

A brilliant New Testament scholar once asked a group of us what is the most important word in the New Testament. We all took stabs at it. Was it love? Faith? Hope? Sanctification? Grace?

"No," he said. "It's the little word *let*. L-E-T." Let Jesus Christ do his good work in you. Let this mind be in you which was also in Christ Jesus. . . . Let your peace return to you. . . . Let your light shine before men. . . . *Let* is a word of transforming faith, with encyclopedias of meaning poured into it. *Let* assumes the total love and power of the Creator. It assumes that heaven is crammed with good gifts the Father wants to give his children. The profoundly simple word *let* is the gate that opens to that power. It gives God permission to work his might in us.

That's the good news. Everything we've talked of so far is not based on sheer effort, once we make the choice to become that person seeking to be more, seeking to live a lifestyle of radical dependence on God, discovering that power within.

There is an incredible power available to us. All you need is what you have—and what you have is what he is! Do you understand the principle? Christ is in you—nothing less than that. You cannot have more, but likewise you need not have less. To put it another way, suppose God were to die tonight. Would it make any difference in the way you live your Christian life tomorrow? Would you notice the difference? Perhaps it depends on who is in the driver's seat, as the following poem so exuberantly expresses:

The Road of Life

At first, I saw God as my observer,
my judge,
keeping track of the things I did wrong,
so as to know whether I merited heaven
or hell when I die.
He was out there sort of like a president.
I recognized His picture when I saw it,
but I really didn't know Him.

But later on
when I met Christ,
it seemed as though life were rather like a bike ride,
but it was a tandem bike,
and I noticed that Christ
was in the back helping me pedal.

I don't know just when it was
that He suggested we change places,
but life has not been the same since.

When I had control,
I knew the way.
It was rather boring,
but predictable . . .
It was the shortest distance between two points.

But when He took the lead,
He knew delightful long cuts,
up mountains,
and through rocky places
at breakneck speeds,
it was all I could do to hang on!
Even though it looked like madness,
He said, "Pedal!"

I worried and was anxious
and asked,
"Where are you taking me?"
He laughed and didn't answer,
and I started to learn to trust.

I forgot my boring life
and entered into the adventure.
And when I'd say, "I'm scared,"
He'd lean back and touch my hand.

He took me to people with gifts that I needed,
gifts of healing,
acceptance
and joy.
They gave me gifts to take on my journey,
my Lord's and mine.

And we were off again.
He said, "Give the gifts away;
they're extra baggage, too much weight."
So I did,
to the people we met,
and I found that in giving I received,
and still our burden was light.

I did not trust Him,
at first,
in control of my life.
I thought He'd wreck it;

but He knows bike secrets,
knows how to make it bend to take sharp corners,
knows how to jump to clear high rocks,
knows how to fly to shorten scary passages.

And I am learning to shut up
and pedal
in the strangest places,
and I'm beginning to enjoy the view
and the cool breeze on my face
with my delightful constant companion, Jesus Christ.

And when I'm sure I just can't do anymore,
He just smiles and says . . . "Pedal."
—author unknown

I wish I could blow every dusty, safe image of the Christian faith from your mind. We are living expressions of the living Christ. He said that we were called to do even greater things than he did. We're called to a life of action, of incarnation, called to *re-present* Jesus in the world continually, not just represent him. Not just be his ambassadors, but re-present *him*. That is plan A.

We may look at each other and roll our eyes and ask, "What's plan B?" But there is no plan B. Watching our fumbling, faltering humanity, God said, "Yes, this is the way I want to continue to express my incarnation in the world. I want to continue to reveal my Son through these people called "Christ-ones." And as Madeleine L'Engle says so well:

In a very real sense not one of us is qualified, but it seems that God continually chooses the most unqualified to do His work, to bear His glory. If we are qualified, we tend to think that we have done the job ourselves. If we are forced to accept our evident lack of qualification, then there's no danger that we will confuse God's work with our own or God's glory with our own.

4
The Essential Need for Change

Has any man ever obtained inner harmony by simply reading about the experiences of others? Not since the world began has it ever happened. Each man must go through the fire himself.
— *Norman Douglas*

A close friend of mine was asked back to his forty-year high school reunion. For months he saved to take his wife back to the place and the people he'd left four decades before. The closer the time came for the reunion, the more excited he became, thinking of all the wonderful stories he would hear about the changes and the accomplishments these old friends would tell him. One night before he left he even pulled out his old yearbooks, read the silly statements and the good wishes for the future that students write to each other. He wondered what ol' Number 86 from his football team had done. He wondered if any others had encountered this Christ who had changed him so profoundly. He even tried to guess what some of his friends would look like, and what kind of jobs and families some of these special friends had.

The day came to leave and I drove them to the airport. Their energy was almost contagious. "I'll pick you up on Sunday evening, and you can tell me all about it," I said. "Have a great time."

Sunday evening arrived. As I watched them get off the plane, my friend seemed almost despondent. I almost didn't want to ask, but finally I said, "Well, how was the reunion?"

"Tim," the man said, "it was one of the saddest experiences of my life."

"Good grief," I said, more than a little surprised. "What happened?"

"It wasn't what happened but what didn't happen. It has been forty years, forty years—and they haven't changed. They had simply gained weight, changed clothes, gotten jobs . . . but they hadn't really changed. And what I experienced was maybe one of the most tragic things I could ever imagine about life. For reasons I can't fully understand, it seems as though some people choose not to change."

There was a long silence as we walked back to the car. On the drive home, he turned to me and said, "I never, never want that to be said of me, Tim. Life is too precious, too sacred, too important. If you ever see me go stagnant like that, I hope you give me a quick, swift kick where I need it—for Christ's sake. I hope you'll love me enough to challenge me to keep growing."

We Are Called to Continual Change

We are called the "resurrection" people. I call it being "Easterized." We are to be transformed—a new "creation" in Christ. And the interesting thing about creation is that it's not something that just happened once and stopped. Creation is a continual happening. It's a process.

Nothing in nature is static. There is a natural need for us to *continue* growing. And when I'm listing reasons why you might consider beginning the process of a peak performance lifestyle, the invitation to the *privilege of growing* is a major one.

Martin Luther King, Jr., once said: "I may not be the man I want to be; I may not be the man I ought to be; I may not be the man I could be; I may not be the man I can be; but praise God, I'm not the man I once was."

This continuing transformation is the central theme of the Old and New Testaments. We grow in Christ.

But it takes courage to grow. The opposite of courage is

not cowardice, but conformity. "Clone-liness," as someone said, is not next to godliness.

But we must grow. And the Holy Sweat concept is one of continued, exciting, life-changing growth that any of us—all of us—can experience.

"I'm a Sinner!"

Not too long ago I bumped into a friend I had worked with in a youth ministry, but had not seen for almost seven years. When I knew this wonderful young woman, she was a solid, creative, capable Christian, one I admired for her maturity. But when I ran into her recently I noticed immediately that she had changed in an astonishing way. You could see it. She radiated a presence of joy, and a sense of peace and certitude. It was quite a startling change. I said to her, "Now, don't take this wrong, but you seem different."

She smiled, and said, "Yes, I am."

I asked, "Well, can you explain to me what brought about this change?"

She said, "I don't think you'd understand."

"I agree, I'm not real bright, but try me anyway," I said.

She explained, "I was rereading Romans one day, and well . . . I discovered I really am a sinner (saved by grace)."

Somewhat shocked, I said, "*That's* the reason you're so peaceful and joyful and calm?"

"Yes."

I said, "Well, you got me. I don't understand. You had to know you're a sinner before you became a Christian."

"Right," she said, "I always knew I was a sinner, but when I became a Christian, I thought I wasn't a sinner anymore. If I blew it, I'd condemn myself for days because I thought, since I was a Christian, I shouldn't be making mistakes anymore."

She was right, of course. We do that to ourselves and each other. When I was teaching at a nearby university, I probably couldn't count the times I heard a student say, "Oh, I thought he or she was a Christian," implying that after our salvation experience we're beyond reproach and not going to make mistakes anymore.

My friend explained that her rereading of Romans had two profound ramifications in her life. "In recognizing that I was a sinner and that I will always be one, I realized again the profound truth of Scripture that tells me that if left to my own devices, left to my own will, I will always choose selfishness and sin. I will always do the wrong thing. *Always*. So when I make mistakes, I now understand that doing so is just the way I'm wired. I'm not surprised. And I stop feeling unnecessarily guilty, letting that false guilt tear me down."

"Now I'm beginning to understand." I said. "You're so right."

"You know what Brother Lawrence answered centuries ago when someone asked him what he did when he sinned?" she asked. "He said, 'I simply ask God for forgiveness and then I continue.' Well, that's what I do now too."

"And the second result?" I said.

"The second result is even more astonishing. I then realized that if I did anything good in my life, it was not really *me* doing it, but God at work in my life. So everytime something good happened in my life, I recognized it was God's grace and God's power. So now I spend my time watching how he works through me, and being thankful and grateful and surprised that he does."

"You look at everything that way?" I asked.

"I see God working in my life all the time. I'm just stunned. I'm changing and growing because God's at work in me. It all began when I recognized that it wasn't me but God doing these good things. And I'm telling you, I've been just overwhelmed by his love and grace. It's real, and it's continuous—and I can see it. So how could I look and feel any other way but this?"

My friend *had* changed. Not from something "bad" to something "good," but from something "good" to something *amazing*. She was a solid, moral Christian before. But after her new understanding, she became ignited, spontaneously combustible in Christ. And now *anything* could happen in her life, and she welcomed it.

Like so many good, decent Christians, she could have lived her whole life without realizing how astonishing the Christian life can be. Instead, she would have lived it hung up on every misconception that filled her with guilt and anxiety. But she found out there was more. And that's the way we can be, too, not merely a flickering candlelight but a Roman candle—ready for anything, and wanting to grow and change.

The best and most wonderful that can happen to you in this life is that you should be silent and let God work and speak.

You are not the oil, you are not the air—merely the point of combustion, the flashpoint where the light is born.
You are merely the lens in the beam. You can only receive, give, and possess the light as a lens does.

—Dag Hammarsjköld, *Markings*

Transformed—Even at Age 82

Is there a time when it's too late to jump into a new dimension in your Christian life? Never. Change is possible anytime in our lives.

An 82-year-old man wrote me not long ago. A pastor for fifty-two years, he was now struggling with skin cancer. It was so bad that he'd already had fifteen skin operations. Besides suffering from the pain, he was so embarrassed about how the cancer had scarred his appearance, that he wouldn't go out. Then one day he was given *You Gotta Keep Dancin'* in which I tell of my long struggle with the chronic, intense pain from a near-fatal climbing accident. In that book, I told of the day when I realized that the pain would be with me forever. At that moment, I made a pivotal decision. I knew that it was up to me to choose how I responded to it. So I chose joy (which we'll discuss at length in the next section).

After reading awhile, the elderly pastor said he put the book down, thinking, "He's crazy. I can't choose joy."

So he gave up on the idea. Then later he read in John 15:11

that joy is a gift. Jesus says, "I want to give you my joy so that your joy may be complete."

A gift! he thought. He didn't know what to do, so he got down on his knees. Then he didn't know what to say, so he said, "Well, then, Lord, *give it to me.*"

And suddenly, as he described it, this incredible hunk of joy came from heaven and landed on him.

"I was overwhelmed," he wrote. "It was like the joy talked about in Peter, a 'joy unspeakable and full of glory.' I didn't know what to say, so I said, 'Turn it on, Lord, turn it on!'" And before he knew it, he was dancing around the house. He felt so joyful that he actually felt born again—again. And this astonishing change happened at the age of 82.

He just had to get out. So much joy couldn't stay cooped up. So he went out to the local fastfood restaurant and got a burger. A lady saw how happy he was, and asked, "How are you doing?"

He said, "Oh, I'm wonderful!"

"Is it your birthday?" she asked.

"No, honey, it's better than that!"

"Your anniversary?"

"Better than that!"

"Well, what is it?" she asked excitedly.

"It's the joy of Jesus. Do you know what I'm talking about?"

The lady shrugged and answered, "No, I have to work on Sundays."

Isn't that the way it is? We've limited the idea of an exciting Christianity to one day of the week! Yet this man was living proof that change can produce a joy that spreads out over all the days of our lives, and it can happen during *any* season or circumstance of life.

5
Our Ultimate Goal: "Wholiness"

Be holy because I am holy.   —1 Peter 1:16

Whether a person arrives at his destiny or not—the place that is peculiarly his or hers—depends on whether or not that person finds the kingdom within and hears the call to wholeness and holiness—or what I would call, "wholiness."

Dietrich Bonhoeffer in his *Letters and Papers from Prison* points out that the Scripture verse, "You therefore, must be perfect, as your heavenly Father is perfect" (Matthew 5:48 RSV) actually means, "You shall be whole [complete]—even as your heavenly father is whole." There is the goal. It is the goal of this peak performance process we are talking about. Christ came to make us whole and holy.

Holiness

Speaking about holiness is somewhat like washing an elephant. You never know where to start. Holiness is not a state to be attained but a never-ending process—the core of which is the quality of our continually growing relationship with and through Christ. Holiness is not a place, a thing, or a building. Holiness is in the journey, the process, a gift.

The traditional meaning of the root word *holy* is "to be set apart for God, distinct, sanctified."

But another meaning of the root of holy is "hale," as in whole, hale, and hearty. It's an aliveness—not just physical health, but a robustness of spirit. Both of these root meanings strongly imply that holiness is a given. We cannot earn it. We don't become holy by acquiring merit badges and Brownie points. It has nothing to do with virtue or job descriptions or morality. It is nothing we can do in this do-it-yourself world. It is gift, sheer gift, waiting there to be recognized and received. We don't have to "be qualified" to be holy.

For me, holiness has always been a distant and rather untouchable concept, a stained-glass image expressed through a detachment and disengagement from the world. I think, without even knowing it, I had adopted a concept of holiness more closely aligned with the Pharisees than with Jesus. But while writing this book, I had a simple but disturbing insight: The holiest person who ever lived was undoubtedly Jesus Christ, and he never separated himself from that which was disgusting or soiled. Rather, he invited those very sectors of life to be redeemed and reclaimed through him. Were these not holy things?

"But what do you do with a man who is supposed to be the holiest man who has ever lived and yet goes around talking with prostitutes and hugging lepers?" as Becky Manley Pippert has put it so well. "What do you do," she asks, "with a man who not only mingles with the most unsavory people but actually seems to enjoy them?"

> The religious accused him of being a drunkard, a glutton and having tacky taste in friends. . . . Jesus was simply not your ideal Rotarian. . . . It is a profound irony that the Son of God visited this planet and one of the chief complaints against him was that he was not religious enough.
>
> The religious of his day were offended because he did not follow their rules and traditions. He was bold and outspoken. He favored extreme change and valued what they felt was insignificant, which was largely the "unlovely". . . .
>
> To say he was not the master of subtlety would be putting it mildly. . . . I think Jesus would have been my

last choice as a speaker for a fund-raising drive. Imagine a scene in which you would gather all the powerful leaders and religious elite so they could hear Jesus give a talk (such as Matthew 23). . . . When they are seated, Jesus comes out and his opening words are "You bunch of snakes. You smell bad. . . . You're hypocrites and blind guides. And I want to thank you very much for coming. . . ." It was not exactly a speech that endeared the Pharisees to Jesus, which was what the disciples pointed out when they told him with a sudden flash of insight, "We think you might have offended them." But for those who loved him he was equally exasperating. He constantly kept smashing some of his own followers' expectations of what the Messiah should do. He simply did not fit their mold. He did not try to. They thought the Messiah would come in power and liberate Jerusalem. . . . But the only power that Jesus demonstrated was the power of servanthood.[5]

A friend tells of a woman addicted to heroin who became a Christian. Thinking about her past and then of her future, the friend asked a profound question about holiness. "If she were to live a thoroughly perfect Christian life for the next hundred years, at what point does her spiritual journey involve holiness? If the changing events in her life are not now holy, when will they be?"

It is vital that we understand that holiness comes with our growing relationship with God and is measured by the degree of our willingness to struggle and serve, by our passionate thirst for life in its truest form, and by our ardent desire to be and become. Holiness concerns itself with the quality of our lives, who and where we are—and where we are going. It concerns our whole being and our whole doing.

Wholiness

There is also a dimension of "wholiness" we don't readily see. God is concerned with all of me, and all of you.

Did you know that the word "salvation" comes from the Latin root word *salus*, which means wholeness? God cares about our intellectual needs, our physical needs, and our emotional needs as well as our spiritual needs. He's committed to the whole person. We, therefore, need to be on a quest to discover and develop our wholeness as well as our holiness.

When Elijah ran off in despair and depression after Jezebel chased him away, he pleaded with God to do something. God could have done something supernatural. Instead, God gave him food and rest, for that's what Elijah needed. His physical needs had to be met before he could continue to be what God called him to be. It's the same with us. We need to be attentive to our wholeness and strive toward it, because as we are whole we are then free to be more effective in the kingdom—free to give ourselves away with reckless abandon.

"Wholiness" is both gift and effort. Just as we don't ask which wing on an airplane is more important, the left one or the right one, we don't ask whether *gift* or *effort* is more essential to "wholiness." Both are needed. The 82-year-old pastor had to *ask* for the gift of joy before receiving it. And my friend who made the effort to dig deeper into Romans had to do that for herself before she gained a life-changing insight. We must make that choice. There is a critical step that has always been up to us.

In my late twenties, a bunch of my friends and I decided to sail around the world. I have to admit, though, at the time I was a bit worried. I hadn't ever sailed before. I was uneasy and anxious. So I spent a lot of time reading the Bible and praying about it, until it dawned on me that God was whispering, "Tim, I'll give you peace if you read some books on sailing. The reason you're anxious is not due to lack of prayer, but to your lack of sailing knowledge."

I wasn't unprayerful; I was unskilled. So I took a step I needed to take to "let" God work his peace in my heart. I began reading about sailing.

We must take that initial effort of getting to the "let." Remember? It's the most important word of the New Testament as the seminary professor explained. When we choose to let Jesus work his good work in us we discover what is already within us—because of Who lives within us. We must open our minds to change, and begin.

Eugene Peterson has said:

> Every Christian's story is a freedom story. Each tells how a person has been set free from the confines of small ideas, from the chains of what other people think, from the emotional cages of guilt and regret, from the prisons of self. . . . We are free to change. The process of that change is always a good story, but is never a neat formula.[6]

We all *are* our own stories. If we allow ourselves to grow and to change, our stories will always be good, and they will always be in our own style, too, with no neat preplanned formulas. We're unique and complex, and so are our stories.

What follows in Part Two are ten ideas to get us thinking about the process of change, on a lifestyle that is the way to "wholiness." This is the *what* of Holy Sweat, a peak performance process that continues to challenge me and others. *God will supply, but we must apply.* The way you apply what you read, the way you integrate the points into your own Christian walk, is your own complex formula. It is *your* own personal story—your process of translating theology into biography—after all.

More than anything these points are an invitation to make that story of yours not just an adventure, but *the* adventure—that lasts and grows and changes and astonishes throughout your whole life.

Interested? If so, has God got a life for you. . . .

PART TWO

THE PERSONAL PEAK PERFORMANCE PROCESS

The "What" of Holy Sweat

I have never met a Christian who sat down and planned to live a mediocre life.

—*Howard Hendricks*

The word 'Christian' means different things to different people. To one person it means a stiff, upright, inflexible way of life, colorless and unbending. To another it means a risky, surprise-filled venture, lived tiptoe at the edge of expectation . . . If we get our information from the biblical material, there is no doubt that the Christian life is a dancing, leaping, daring life.

—*Eugene Peterson*

Son, you know God created everything—except one thing. Do you know what that is? . . . a substitute for experience. God created everything except a *substitute* for experience.

—*Gino the cook*

We are human becomings . . . .

No, that's not a typographical error. We really aren't so much human beings as human *becomings*. Everyday we are becoming the person we will be. Some people will become *less* than they are now by the time the next week, the next year and the next decade rolls around. But most of us want to become *more*.

To do that I believe we need a guide of some sort through which the Holy Spirit can begin his work, a set of keys or holy "cues" to get us jump-started and moving on. With that sort of help, we can be on our way to being a "peak performer"—becoming the very best we can be—for a very unselfish reason.

Does that sound like your average peak performance concept? I hope not, because as I've said before, this is not a motivational book in the normal sense of the term. *Holy Sweat* is about a different sort of peak performance—an ongoing, daily, spiritual process whose aim is far greater than a trophy for the mantle.

PEAK PERFORMANCE KEYS (pēēk pür · for · mŭnz kēēz)
1. *n.* small tools which have the ability to unlock doors to a person's untapped capabilities leading to previously unknown dimensions of character.
2. *v.* the process of putting the following into personal dynamic action.

Some of us involved with Summit Expedition wear T-shirts that proclaim in big bold letters: "The Journey Continues. . . ." The following points, I think, are best described as steps—not toward a predefined destination but as a balanced way of traveling that ongoing Journey.

What do I mean by that? First, it is by walking that one creates the path. Second, I want you to think of these ideas as interconnected, dependent on one another—like taking a step with your left and then the next with your right, alternating from one to the other in a sort of rhythm that gives balance and direction.

Because our Peak Performance Journey is an ongoing one, the balance these points offer *as a whole* is vital in keeping that Journey continuing. We need them all. When we've lost our courage, we find that our passion for excellence is sparse. When our passion for excellence is low, then our vision is hazy. When we're low on joy, we find the entire process tedious and unfulfilling.

In other words, without the balance of *all* the points, we find ourselves hopping one-legged instead of striding confidently. Then the Journey becomes a jerky, grit-your-teeth effort instead of a Spirit-filled, confident pilgrimage toward being our very best in and for our Creator.

We are all "becoming" something. Through the following ideas, that "becoming" can be something very, very special—for ourselves and for the world around us.

6
You Gotta Start

Fear not that your life shall come to an end, but rather that it shall never have a beginning.

—*John Henry Newman*

Don't wait. You'll end up waiting forever . . . jump into the now.

—*Clyde Reid*

Even if you are on the right track, you will get run over if you just sit there.

—*Will Rogers*

This may sound crazy, but before anything can happen, before you can accomplish any process of change, you must be willing to get off the dime and start. You've got to get off high center. You've got to quit planning and thinking and wishing, and jump headlong into doing. It may surprise you to find out that this one point is the biggest stumbling block for most people.

Paul Tournier said, "The greatest tragedy in life is that most people spend their entire lives *indefinitely preparing to live.*"

To me, the saddest phrases in the English language are "if only" or "it might have been." The majority of us whisper these two phrases most of our lives, because we can't make ourselves take that first step. "It's such a risk," we may think. "I'm just not the type."

But as Samuel Johnson said, "Nothing will ever be attempted if all possible objections must first be overcome."

And why are we so hesitant? Two reasons are our propensity

for self-limitation and our fear of making mistakes. Afraid to step into the unknown, we inadvertently put life on hold, saying, "I just can't risk it." Underestimating ourselves, thinking ourselves weak, we hold ourselves back, saying "I just can't do it." But, we must never affirm such self-limitations. To begin anything new we usually have to throw out those preconceived notions of what we can and cannot do. We have to get rid of old images we've attached to ourselves: "I've never been a good problem solver." "I've never been a gentle person." "I'm not an athlete."

When we hang on to such notions, we put a lid on our ability to change, our ability to discover our true potential, before we've even had an opportunity to change. And when we do, we take away the leverage to bring about any change, placing ourselves in our own preconceived prisons. The ultimate tragedy, as Oliver Wendell Holmes has said, is that many people go to their graves with their music still in them.

Think back, though, to one of the essential themes of this book: The Christian life is not what it seems. We need to let go of our old images of faith as well as our old images of ourselves. We need to rethink who we are and what being a Christian truly means. We need to throw out our puny images. The Christian life is not supposed to be tidy, neat, prepackaged, and hermetically sealed. The truth is that life is ambiguous, unpredictable, untidy, messy, and often, quite hard. The fiery Zorba the Greek says, "Life *is* trouble. Only death is not. To be alive means to buckle our belt and *look* for trouble." Our Christianity gives us the strength, guidance, and reason to handle it. When we impose a canned and neat and perfect image on our living, that image can often keep us from starting anything that doesn't likewise sound as canned and neat and perfect. It's not that we don't have good intentions.

It's interesting that the word *intention* comes just before *inter* in the dictionary, and inter means "to bury." How many of our dreams are often buried by mere good intentions: "I was going to . . ." "I almost . . ." "I intended to . . ." That's

70

why boldness has genius and magic in it. The greatest act of courage is the first step.

Beginning is so hard it is almost literally true that to start means you're halfway there. Maybe it's even more. Woody Allen once quipped that 80 percent of success is showing up. Who knows how many great projects never succeeded because people never had the courage to begin them.

There actually is a fact of physics in such an idea. The momentum factor plays a large part in accomplishing any goal. Think of a locomotive. When it's stopped, you can put several small blocks of wood underneath its wheels and they will keep it stopped even though its engines are revved up. Think how a train starts; it's a slow-going process. It picks up speed very, very slowly. Yet once that train is moving, it can actually go through several feet of steel-reinforced concrete. That's the power of getting started, of momentum.

Our lives are controlled by inertia. If we are living life with a block of wood holding us in place, we tend to stay there. But, just as in physics, if we are put into motion, we tend to stay in motion. I hate to imagine how much potential for good has gone down the drain because it was never able to break through the strain of inception.

Are you suffering from analysis paralysis? You can think far too long on a thing—so much so, that you never act. Without realizing it you can become one of God's "frozen chosen."

There is an eloquence in action. *It is easier to act your way into a new way of thinking than it is to think your way into a new way of acting.*

But I can hear you thinking, *Oh, you don't know my circumstances. I'm too old to change.* Or, *my background limits me.* It's a natural reaction, this making of excuses. Most of us tend to resist change and hence get bogged down in our own inertia. I was once told that the definition of a coward is a person who makes a lot of excuses. Ever since I heard that I've been much more aware of using excuses, especially for inaction. One of the greatest things I know about being justified in Christ is that it sets me free from constantly having to justify myself. I'm free to explore, discover, change—to act!

In 1982, the book *In Search of Excellence* caused a revolution in American business thought, selling five million copies in fifteen languages. The book focused on eight attributes that are essential for excellence in a company. The first of the book's attributes for peak performance in business was "a bias for action." Any of us who are going to be productive, who are considering the process of personal peak performance as a lifestyle, must have that same "bias for action." I've got a friend who consistently says, "Do *something* even if it's wrong." As the old saying goes, it's easier to ask forgiveness than permission. Having a bias for action means taking that chance.

In rock climbing there is a technical term called a "commitment move." Often it's the crux move of the climb. Handholds seem scarce and footholds appear nonexistent. The tendency is to "bogart"—to freeze, to panic, to wait until exhaustion causes you, the climber, to quit the climb. You have a rope around you that will keep you from ever falling more than a few inches. But still, your first feeling is to bogart. On our Summit Expedition courses, the staff will constantly encourage the climber to "go for it." "Don't bogart! Give it your best shot!" And on a commitment move, you've either got to go for it or come off the climb.

What's your commitment move these days?

We must realize that risk is at the very core of the Christian life. You're not called to be safe from all life's troubles, simply secure in the knowledge that you're "roped to" the living Christ. His rope is trustworthy and time-tested. The only thing about life that is permanent is change. If we stay on that ledge, forever expecting the next handhold to be easy and guaranteed, we'll never go anywhere. Sometimes what is waiting is difficult; sometimes it's surprising; often it's unpredictable. But we can't let that keep us from moving, from trying.

I believe that if God speaks to us anywhere, he speaks to

us in our daily lives, in an ordinary setting. We can't wait for lightning to strike or for the wind to die down before we step out to make ourselves all we can be. The necessary move is called a step, or leap, of faith for a very good reason. As we step out, God will reveal himself more with every step along the way, because it's much easier to steer a moving vehicle than one that is parked.

Clyde Reid, in his book *Celebrate the Temporary*, says, "Don't wait. You'll end up waiting forever. Celebrate the now with all its pain and difficulties. . . . But also celebrate the wonder of being alive. You and I are living miracles. So jump into the now and begin the process." You don't have forever to fulfill your dreams. Forget the past. Embrace the future. Start. Now.

The great tragedy of today's convenient world is that you can live a *trivial* life and get away with it.

I would hate to get to the end of my life and realize I had not lived, that I'd never dared to take a chance to love, to explore, to realize my best. Maybe the greatest risk in life is to not risk. We should ask ourselves what our lives will be like if we don't risk beginning.

Once you've mustered the courage to step into the unknown, you will have had a taste of the momentum and it will be easier to start again, and again. We all must continually struggle to overcome our doubts and hesitations. All of us have at some point in our lives surmounted powerful obstacles in life, and gone on to accomplish seemingly impossible things. As one writer put it,

For a long time
  it had seemed to me that life was about to begin—
  real life.
But there was always some obstacle in the way.
Something to be got through first,
  some unfinished business;
  time still to be served,
  a debt to be paid.

73

Then life would begin.
At last it dawned on me that these obstacles were my life.
—B. Howland

The sad part is that most people sit around and wait for life to come to them. Have you ever thought what your life would be like if you had never taken a risk? You probably would have never learned to walk, never moved away from home, never made a friend, and never really gone anywhere or done anything the least bit memorable. The truth is, we cannot grow without taking risks, without loosening our grip on the known and the certain, and taking a chance in reaching for a little bit more of life. Some people are content with mere routine, a revolving-door existence of waking up, eating breakfast, going to work, coming home, going to bed. But others seem infected with a rage to live. Their secret is that they are always beginning something new.

Above everything, the greatest commitment move is *always* that of beginning, taking that very important first step. Life is not meant to be a spectator sport. Even a small step is a step, but the first step is the hardest and most important. Without it, nothing else can ever happen.

I heard a story of a man who loaned a book to a friend. When the book was returned, the man noticed that on many of the pages there appeared the three letters, "YBH," written in pencil in the margin. Obviously curious, he asked his friend the meaning of YBH.

"Oh, I thought the book was terrific," the friend said. "In fact, it could have been life-changing." The YBH in the margins stood for "Yes, But How?" So here are a few practical suggestions that I hope will be of some help:

• Start NOW . . . literally. "If you don't get started in the next seventy-two hours," one very wise man has said, "you ain't gonna get started at all."

• Don't wait for all the problems to get solved, for all the obstacles to be removed, for the earth, sun, and the stars to line up perfectly. You'll be waiting forever.

• Struggle is okay. So is doubt. If you stop struggling, you stop life. Jump in anyway.

• Never affirm self-limitations. The One who lives within you is greater than those obstacles outside of you.

• Change your language. Don't say, "I *have* to!" because that automatically produces resistance from within. Say instead, "I *choose* to!" I guarantee this subtle change of language will have powerful results.

• "We cannot change anything unless we first accept it. Condemnation does not liberate, it oppresses" (C. G. Jung). Accept fully who you are and where you are—and then, by choice, develop a proactive strategy for change.

• Get a friend to help you start. Encouragement is one of the most powerful tools in the universe.

• Don't take yourself so seriously! The reason angels fly is because they take themselves so lightly. As John Powell reminds us, "he who has learned to laugh at himself shall never cease to be entertained." Genuine laughter, at ourselves, especially, gives us great strength to start anew. In laughter and lightheartedness there is freedom.

• Act "as if"—you were going to change history by courageously starting—because, in a very subtle way, you are.

• Don't make excuses. Period!

• Try not to interfere with God. The "Allness" of God wants to move powerfully through our "eachness." Don't frustrate the God process. Find your own unique way of "letting" him express this fullness in you.

• Perhaps one of the unforgivable sins is to give up on ourselves and God. Hold a cup under an opened faucet and it will quickly fill. The process is slightly more difficult if you hold your cup upside down. *So, turn your cup right side up.*

• Act as if it were impossible to fail.

- Stop worrying and start believing. You can't worry and praise God at the same time.
- Here are a few practical words from a Book I've been reading lately. By the way, it has a dynamite ending:
    —"And my God will supply every need of yours according to his riches. . . ."
    —"Do not be anxious about your life. . . ."
    —"It is your Father's good pleasure to give you the kingdom."
    —"But seek first his kingdom and . . . all these things shall be yours as well."
    —"As he thinketh in his heart, so is he."
    —"Lord, I believe; help thou mine unbelief!"
    —"So faith . . . if it has no works, is dead."
    —"If God is for us, who is against us?"
    —"Ask, and it will be given you; seek, and you will find; knock, and it will be opened to you."
    —"Whatever you ask in prayer, *believe* that you receive it, and you will." [7]

I can say with great certainty that you'll never get to where you want to be unless you let go of where you are now. The only thing sadder than a work unfinished is a work never begun.

7
Vision

Is life so wretched?
Isn't it rather your hands which are too small
    your vision which is muddled?
You are the one who must grow up!

—*Dag Hammarskjöld*

There is no magic in small plans. When I consider my ministry, I think of the world. Anything less than that would not be worthy of Christ nor His will for my life.

—*Henrietta Mears*

Your old men shall dream dreams
    your young men shall see visions   —Joel 2:28

To make the process of peak performance real in your life, you must have vision. Having your own vision opens you to God's possibilities. It takes the cobwebs off your dreams and highlights the fact that your life is one of God's incredible investments in the future.

Many people say, "If I see it, I'll believe it." I think they've got it backwards.

In truth if you can believe it, you can see it.

The vision always comes first. In a way, it's like walking down the street. You know something lies around the corner. But until you get to the corner, you really cannot know the possibilities waiting there. Unless you have a vision for those possibilities waiting there, you may never make the effort to walk to that corner to find out.

Most of us know that our potential is untapped and undiscovered. But until we have a vision that more is possible in life than what we ordinarily perceive, then it will remain unused and unrecognized. In *The Secret of Staying in Love*, John Powell writes:

Very few of us ever even approach the realization of our full potential. I accept the estimate that the average person accomplishes only 10 percent of his promise . . . sees only 10 percent of the beauty around him, hears only 10 percent of the music and poetry of the universe, and smells only a tenth of the world's fragrance and tastes only a tenth of the deliciousness of being alive. He is only open to 10 percent of his emotions, tenderness, wonder and awe. His mind embraces only a small part of the thoughts, reflections and understanding of which he is capable. . . . He will die without ever having really lived or really loved. To me, this is the most frightening of all possibilities. . . . I would hate to think that you or I might die without ever having *really* loved or really *lived*. (Italics mine)[8]

How is your life going these days? Are you going for it with everything you've got? Do you have a big vision of what life can be for you? Are you taking it head-on or head-down? Are you gazing at the stars and the road ahead or merely watching for the cracks in the sidewalk? Many of us never stop to think about it. We just exist, going through the motions. We're not even really conscious of being alive. For God's sake, literally, we need to stop and consider how our lives are doing. We need to match them up to what we want to do and be.

Too many of us, though, are like some of the students I had when I was teaching in high school. Those young people were so apathetic that they made sheep look like they were taking pep pills. One morning, I got so frustrated with the attitude of all those kids that in my first-period psychology class I walked up to the blackboard and wrote APATHY in huge letters three feet high across the whole board. A senior sitting on the front row leaned back, looked up, and began to mouth the letters. Here was this eighteen-year-old, the culmination of our formal educational process about to be set loose on society, spelling the word out loud, letter by letter, not once but twice: "A . . . P . . . A . . . T . . . H . . . Y" Finally he said, "A-PAY-THEE—now what the heck is that anyway?" I was just about to let him have it when a guy sitting next to him, slumped in his chair as well, leaned over and said, "Who cares?"

The Bible says that without a vision the people will atrophy. They will wither and die. They will not fulfill their full promise. Without a vision of the type of person you want to become, of the things you want to do as you join the process of peak performance, your dreams and sense of aliveness will perish.

Where does such vision come from?

Charlie Shedd wrote once, "Lord, help me understand what you had in mind when you made the original me." Our visions come from what God has in mind for us. He doesn't see us with all the self-imposed limitations we've put on ourselves. He sees us packed with potential and an incredible ability to change and grow, in every area and effort of our lives. That vision may change and grow as you do, as God is unpredictable and amazing. But having that vision is all-important. Leaving the specifics and the corrections of direction to God is part of the secret.

Phillipians 2:13 says that God is at work within you, giving you the will and the power to achieve his purpose.

Still, many of us have a hard time truly forming our inner vision. Maybe the problem is we're taking ourselves and our lives too seriously. Does that sound crazy? Isn't the whole idea to take ourselves seriously enough to begin the process of a peak per-formance lifestyle? Well, yes and no. We are to take our potential seriously, but never ourselves. When we take ourselves too seri-ously, we become self-absorbed, self-conscious, and more open to the opinions of others than the inner vision we have hiding within us. And such self-absorption will defeat the process quicker than anything. We are to take God seriously, but never ourselves. Likewise, because God takes us so seriously, we are free not to take ourselves so seriously.

How, then, do we cultivate this inner vision? How do you identify your unique purpose, your compelling mission that will fuel that dream? Here are two possible starting points for discovering your personal vision.

Ask yourself two questions:

1. What do you love to do?

What are you crazy about? What would you like to spend all your time doing if you had the chance? Look hard at those things and they will tell you much about the shape of your vision.

Part of this adventure you're invited on is the adventure of understanding your true gifts and all they say about you and what God has in mind for you. Just as Charlie Shedd prayed, we need to find out what God had in mind when he thought of the original "us." It's possible. In fact, to have an inner vision is critical if we're going to live our lives to the fullest.

The good news is that you have the answer with you all the time. Where? God's imprinted it, stamped it on your being. Elizabeth O'Connor, in her book, *Eighth Day of Creation*, explains: "We ask to know the will of God without guessing that his will is written into our very beings. We perceive that will when we discern our gifts. Our obedience and surrender to God is in large part our obedience and surrender to our gifts."

The psalmist prayed that God would give us the desires of our hearts (Psalm 20:4). He's placed the desire there. Do you love words? Numbers? Music? The out-of-doors? Working with people? Your gifts, your talents, your vision, and God's will for you are hidden there waiting to be discovered.

Summit Expedition is I'm sure a part of my vision. I love physical things, I love working with people, and I love the idea of helping people discover themselves. For several years I found I could do all those things through coaching. But as I grew, I found that I wanted to work with a wider range of kids. What about those kids who are so uncoordinated that they have trouble tying their shoes? They too have limitless abilities that need to be tapped. And what about troubled kids and handicapped kids. They too need to recognize and *experience* how unique and special they are. And that's exactly what happens when we take these kids, and now adults as well, on our trips.

When I began Summit Expedition I had no previous experience or particular aptitude for rock climbing. I had never done it until I was in my thirties. I started Summit primarily for educational and ministry reasons, not mountaineering reasons. But I knew my vision of ministering to people in a creative environment would mesh with my love of the outdoors in some way and Summit Expedition was the answer. I was challenged to learn everything necessary (and have enjoyed the process immensely); Summit Expedition's technical standards as well as ministry standards are very high. In fact, in the seventeen years of our existence, we've never had an accident of consequence. We tell people that our programs are safer than being on the freeway. And they are.

The psalmist says, "May he grant you your heart's desire, and fulfil all your plans! May we shout for you over your victory, and in the name of our God set up banners!" (Psalm 20:4, 5). We know that God wants us to be who we are, and to do what we love to do and are called to do. There is no greater satisfaction and joy than that of doing what you were intended to do. He wants us to find our special abilities and then invest them in the world. Writer Frederick Buechner says, "The place God calls you to is the place where your deep gladness and the world's deep hunger meet."

It's important that each of us looks beyond the obvious for our gifts. You may have an unusual ability. Maybe it's even something as important as listening. I have seen more lives changed by a quality listener than I have by a quality speaker. But your special abilities *are* there, waiting to be acknowledged.

Remember the verse in Proverbs that says to train up a child in the way he should go and when he is older he will not depart from it? In the Hebrew, the actual meaning is much more than just encouraging a child to be religious. It implies that parents are to help their children (1) discover their unique gifts God has given them and (2) find the place in the world where they can use those special gifts and abilities. When they're older, they will continue in their unique expression and explanation of God's will for them.

What do you love to do? It says so much about you and your potential for shaping the future.

2. Who are your heroes?

Actually, the question should not be *who are your heroes*, but, *what do you consider heroic?* What are those qualities you see in others that you passionately admire? Spending some time with this question is a great way of knowing what values really touch you and what your vision for living might be.

One of my heroes is the fictional character Zorba the Greek. If you recall the character, he was a man who lived life passionately, with such reckless abandonment that he saw everything as if for the first time, deliciously savoring each moment. His way of living was contagious. Zorba danced whenever his grief or problems overwhelmed him. His zest for life at its fullest, his amazing way of flowing with life and pain inspired his employer, whom he called "Boss," to say to him, "Zorba, teach me to dance." Zorba had an incredible appetite for life and grace. I've found that infectious. As Zorba said so well: "The life of a man is a road with steep rises and dips. All sensible people use their brakes. But I did away with my brakes altogether a long time ago, because I'm not at all scared of a jolt. . . . what have I got to lose? Nothing. Even if I do take it easy, won't I end up the same? Of course I will. So, let's scorch along. Every man has his folly, but the greatest folly of all, in my view, is not to have one."

I think of Albert Schweitzer who gave up so much to give so much to the people of Africa. I think of Martin Luther King, Jr., a unique example of the power of servant leadership. I think of Mother Teresa with her vision for the untouchables and the dying in the gutters of Calcutta, a vision for which she sacrifices so much with such joy that she has captured the hearts of the world. And I think of Joni Eareckson Tada who has the vision of enabling handicapped people to realize how much they have to give.

Many of my heroes are people who are living very ordinary lives but are doing so in heroic ways. I know single mothers who are doing their best to raise their families against incredible odds. I think of my handicapped friends whom I admire for their amazing tenacity and courage and laughter in the midst of difficulties. And I think of my wife who went back to college after turning forty to gain her degree, and is now working on a master's degree while taking care of two boys.

I think of Bill Milliken who is a man who leaks at the seams with Christ's love. He was introduced not too long ago as "a living, registered, bonafide burning bush." Today he has developed one of the finest programs in the country dealing with urban high school dropouts. He's shared with the President, countless heads of state, top officials and businessmen all over the country, his love for inner-city kids who would not otherwise make it. His "Cities in Schools" program is a model for the future, yet he was a college dropout himself.

I think of Craig Schindler whose vision is to make people aware of the frightening possibilities of our nuclear age. He has a Ph.D. and a law degree, and could be making money hand over fist, but he's so concerned with the nuclear issue and its impact on humanity that he lives on a shoestring in order to support his "Project Victory," a vision of the triumph of human intelligence and spirit over the forces that threaten our future. He sees a vision of a time of peace and human dignity—and has already developed a reconciling process where everyone can win.

I think of John McEntyre who has a vision for being a wonderful husband and dad and someday infusing the depth of his Christian beliefs into the width of his humanities studies—to teach in a new and exciting way.

And I think of Jesus. Most people wouldn't consider him a

hero, since he's our Savior. But Jesus epitomizes the values of God, and he demonstrated in his life the quiet heroics of a lifestyle of wholeness. Courage, gentleness, initiative, simplicity, compassion . . . his are the values I want most in my life. He gives me the best and clearest vision.

Some visions are large. Some are small. None is greater than that of another. Lives are always, and only, changed one-at-a-time, no matter what the vision.

My vision has been somehow to combine adventure and compassion in such a way as to help as many people as possible discover their full potential. I want them to know the joy that transcends all understanding and circumstances. That vision is an expression not only of who I am, but also of who I'm becoming, who I want to be.

Our lives are worth investing—and we'll never know the many ways God wants to use us until we do. We need to be people of compelling mission and great hope who see and do the impossible. I would challenge us all to be people of that kind of contagious vision that transforms our lives and others. Perhaps we need a little "heir conditioning," wherein we remember again and again the King we serve, and that our work represents not only who we are but *whose* we are.

He who is narrow of vision cannot be big of heart. As Winston Churchill once said, "Play for more than you can afford to lose; let your reach exceed your grasp; *then* you will know the rules."

8
Clear, Precise, Written Goals

To move in the dark is to move blindfold.

—1 John 2:11 (PHILLIPS)

Most people don't know what they really want—
but they're sure they haven't got it.

—Alfred E. Newman

The greatest thing in the world is not so much where we stand as in what direction we're moving.

—Oliver Wendell Holmes

If having a vision is mandatory for the peak performance lifestyle, then writing down precise goals is crucial. "Aim at nothing and you'll probably hit it," some witty person once said. It was probably the same person who said, "If you don't know where you're going, you'll probably end up somewhere else." Likewise, if you don't boldly choose your own goals, you are destined to accept someone else's goals. The insight of those one-liners is apparent, we'd all agree. But very few of us take the time to write down specific goals for where we want to end up. Hazy goals inevitably produce hazy results.

Yet that is exactly what we need to do. We need to write down *clearly defined, vividly imagined goals that are packed with emotion*. Why emotion? Because emotion gives our goals power. The more vividly you pack your goals with emotion, the more power they have to propel you.

A couple of years ago, my friend Jim Wilson and I decided to compete in a triathlon, a three-part (swimming, running, and cycling) endurance race. We knew exactly what we were getting into, and more than a few of our friends and those in our families questioned our intelligence. But a triathlon offered an intriguing sort of goal. We knew exactly the distances we had to swim, cycle, and run, so we could train in a very specified fashion for them.

Don't get the wrong idea. A great athlete, I'm not. And I may be one of the world's slowest swimmers. I'll never forget when Jim and I started training. He mentioned that he didn't swim so well, and I said, "You haven't seen me yet." When he lapped me twice in the pool, he stopped and laughed, "You really *are* bad."

But we did it anyway. One of my goals was just to finish; in peak performance, you're struggling to be *your* best, not necessarily *the* best.

During the swimming part of the race, I was so slow that the lifeguard once thought I was a buoy. He wasn't sure I was moving. By the time I finally got out of the water, something like six hundred people were ahead of me and very few were behind me. But I went on. And I finished. I'll never forget the feeling of completing that triathlon. What a great sense of accomplishment—all because I had focused all my energies on one goal.

Norman Vincent Peale tells a story about a frustrated young man who once consulted him about his repeated failures.

"Success completely eludes me," he said. "I wanted to get somewhere."

"Good," Peale replied, "and exactly where do you want to get?"

His reply was a masterpiece of inconclusiveness: "Well, I don't know for sure; never figured that one out. But I'm not happy the way it is. I want to get somewhere."

"Well, what can you do best? What particular skills do you possess?"

"I don't believe I have any particular skills," the man said. "In fact, I have no idea what I'm cut out for or what I can do best."

Peale tried again: "Let me ask you, what would you like to do? If you were told you could have any job you wanted or any achievement, what would you choose?"

"I can't tell you, really," the man replied, somewhat desperately. It was obvious that a minor motivation, if not a strong one, was working within this somewhat confused young man, but it lacked cohesion, sharpness, objectivity.

Peale then responded, "Look—you must fix on a goal, then sharpen and clarify it. Hold it in your conscious mind until it sinks by a process of intellectual and spiritual osmosis into your subconscious. Then you will have it *because it will have you,* all of you. You will begin to move toward that goal on a direct road, not a vague 'somewhere.'"

Human beings are teleological in design. We are all goal-oriented mechanisms, and we all respond to them. One reason so many people live unproductive lives, often feeling lost and without purpose, is that they don't have clear, precise, written goals for themselves which they refer to and amend continually.

Do the goals have to be written down?

To be their most effective, they definitely do. A goal not written down is a wish. That may seem like a lot of trouble, but it is the key to the way the power works. Those goals before you will pull you along like a magnet. The act of writing them down is a commitment to clarity. Seeing them is the first step toward making them reality. Yet *less than 2 percent* of our society has goals written down. I guarantee that if you write down your goals and keep them close at hand, they will focus you. Strong and organized purposefulness toward a definite goal will focus your power and provide the critical motivation to complete them.

Think about it this way. You can put your hand quite close to a light bulb without burning it. That's because the light is diffused. But if you focus that light energy as with a laser beam, you would be crazy to put your hand in front of it. A laser beam can go through eighteen inches of solid steel. The difference is in the focused energy.

That's what goals are—focused energy. They give us a way of taking our incredible gifts plus our inner vision and aiming them both in a precise direction.

Your goals can be designed in three categories: long-term, short-term, and mid-term. Anything over a month is a mid-term goal. Anything less is short-term. And most experts suggest that long-term goals shouldn't really go past one to three years. Life is moving too fast, changes are taking place too quickly. You can look at these goals in this way:

In the above diagram, you'll notice that lifetime goals obviously go right at the very front, at the apex of the arrow. But lifetime goals can also be short-term. In fact, if stated correctly, they should. In some way, you almost have to participate in your lifetime goals *now* for them to ever become reality later.

For instance, one of my lifetime goals is to "make the invisible Christ visible." I can do that now. How I participate in it today also propels me toward it tomorrow and the next day. It's somewhat of a "lifestyle long-term" goal. It's at the front and at the end of my arrow. Another of my lifetime goals is to raise my two boys into free, strong, and committed young people, living out their own unique gifts. That goal I have to do now, or it will not happen later.

As for refining the goals, the long-terms may not need constant attention, but the rest of your goals must be continually refined. An article entitled "How to Stop Wasting Time— Experts' Advice," in a 1982 edition of *U.S. News & World*

Report, contained an interview with R. James Steffen.[9] This time-management expert gave suggestions on how to manage time, be more productive, and perform better. He said that the first principle is to write down goals clearly and precisely. His second principle was to rewrite, redefine, and refine those goals. And his third principle was to rewrite those goals, refine them again, and more carefully analyze them so the individual knows exactly what he or she wants to do. His first three goals all had to do with setting and clarifying goals.

I must confess that at one time in my life I became weary of goal-setting. Then a few years ago I found out something about how the body works that has changed my mind forever. It's called the reticular activating system and is an actual network of cells at the base of the skull that works like a built-in radar system. However, there's a slight catch to it. The network only works if the individual sets a goal. The moment you set your mind on something, the reticular activating system operates to screen out information, excluding all that is unimportant and irrelevant. Hence it helps you focus on the subjects most critical to the mental image.

· You use it consistently, but as with many of the wonders of the human body, you may only rarely notice it. Have you ever been thinking about buying a certain brand of car, for instance, and had the strange sensation of seeing that particular car everywhere—in ads, on television, on the street, everywhere? That model was always there, but suddenly your reticular activating system is at work and you're noticing things you ignored before. It's like deciding to buy a sofa and becoming all excited about it. As you are casually glancing through the newspaper, you notice a half-price sale on sofas. What a coincidence, you think! But the reason you found the information is that you had set the goal of buying a sofa. Otherwise, you'd never have given such an ad a second thought.

The information is there. The chances for our vision to become reality are there. But until we set our goals consciously, our unconscious resources cannot help us. Our vision becomes reality through goals.

Lou Tice, a pioneer in some of the newest thinking on the power of goal-setting, tells this story: He thought he would set a goal to make his wife an art studio out of brick. But brick was hard to find where he lived, so he almost decided against it. Then he remembered the great underlying principle of all goal-setting. A person must form his or her "beliefs without evidence," which simply means to set one's goal clearly based upon what he or she wants, regardless of whether or not the resources appear within reach to attain it. The idea is not to decide in the beginning whether or not a thing can be done, but to set the goal and see what happens. So Lou Tice set the goal.

That morning, as every morning, he had a thirty-minute drive to work. On his way, he drove to the first stop light and for no apparent reason he found his head turning to his left. There was a building being torn down, a brick building. He had driven by that building at least two hundred times and had never noticed the brick.

He drove another few miles and stopped at another light. Glancing to the right he noticed that a shopping center was being torn down. Bricks were everywhere.

He kept driving and as he reached the downtown area, he noticed that the domed stadium he passed everyday was being renovated. It too was made out of bricks. He was overwhelmed. The brick had been there yesterday, all along his drive to and from home. But he had ignored it so well that the night before he had absolutely convinced himself that no bricks were available. The moment his reticular activating system clicked on, though, the bricks he needed were virtually everywhere.

The latest authorities I have read believe that to visualize a goal already fulfilled and to pack that picture with vivid emotion is one of the most successful ways of reaching a goal.

Our minds work on the principle of "dominant image." People have actually been doing this for years, but now that research has made this information available to us, countless stories have confirmed this vital truth about the power of visualization. Consider, for example, the following stories:

In his book, *Releasing Your Brakes*, James Newman tells the story of Bill, a young soldier severely injured in the Korean War. For weeks, Bill was paralyzed, unable to move any muscles except his eyes and jaw. For him to read, a nurse would place a book on a rack over his bed and turn the pages for him. Undaunted, Bill had an idea. He had always wanted to learn to type, so he asked for a typing textbook, and quickly began to memorize the typewriter keyboard. In his imagination, he visualized his fingers actually touching the proper keys and typing words on paper. Without moving a muscle, while lying in a hospital bed, Bill practiced "typing" fifteen to twenty minutes a day.

Finally, after extensive therapy, Bill could move his arms and hands. So he asked to be taken to a hospital office to use a typewriter. In his very first attempt at using the touch-typing skill he had visualized, he typed fifty-five words a minute, with no errors.

In *Say Yes to Your Potential*, Skip Rose tells another story of an experiment done with six basketball teams. All six teams were told to shoot one hundred free throws and record their percentage of goals. Two teams, then, were told to spend several hours a day for two weeks practicing to make their percentage better. Two other teams were sent onto the basketball court and told to spend half the time practicing free throws, attempting to improve on the percentage of shots each scored out of one hundred tries. For the other half of the time, they were told to sit and practice free throws in their imaginations.

The last two teams were told to do nothing except practice over and over in their imaginations. But they were helped with how to visualize and emotionalize the process. A specific scenario was suggested, Ross continues:

> Imagine you are standing at the free throw line. The ball game is over, but you were fouled at the buzzer. Your team trails by one point, and you have two free throws. If you

make them, your team wins the championship of your league. Feel yourself come to the line, bouncing the ball, calming yourself down. Then feel the release of the ball as you shoot and watch the perfect arch as it swishes through the net. The crowd explodes; the game is tied. You are so excited you can hardly contain yourself. You take the ball, you bounce it once, and then you throw it—and it swishes through the net again. The cheers are deafening as the crowd rushes out onto the floor, picks you up and carries you, the hero, away!

For two weeks all six teams practiced as they were told and at the end of that time the teams were tested again for their free-throwing abilities. The first two teams, that had practiced the entire two weeks, only increased their average by about 1 percent. The teams that were told to practice half the time and image half the time increased by the same 1 percent. But the teams that infused their imagining with emotions increased their percentages 4 1/2 percent.

Studies actually show that a vividly imagined goal is as powerful as reality itself. "Imagination is more important than knowledge," said Albert Einstein. The power of writing down your goals and visualizing them cannot be overestimated.

Writing down goals, continually reshaping them, and thinking about them may sound like work. But when they are tied up with your vision, your dreams, about the things you love to do and want to do, they easily become part of the path to the dream. And they never seem like work again. If you don't set your own goals, you will always be accepting other people's goals.

Let me ask you a very simple but profound question: *What is it that you really want out of life?* Why don't you go ahead and plan for it? Our ultimate goal in our peak performance process, as we've said, is wholeness. Living your vision, the *you* God originally had in mind, is wholeness. And what better mental picture to vividly imagine than that?

9
Courage

What we need now is *endless* courage. —*Katherine Porter*

Be strong and of good courage. . . . —Joshua 1:6

One man with courage makes a majority. —*Andrew Jackson*

The trick is not to rid your stomach of butterflies, but to make them fly in formation. —source unknown

We've talked about goals and vision. But what turns goals and vision into reality?

Courage. Courage is the bridge between good ideas and action. We all know that faith is the substance of hope. Well, I believe that courage is the substance of faith. More than that, I'm convinced that love without courage is mere sentimentality—and vision without courage will never be more than a nice dream.

Courage is perhaps one of the most misunderstood and underrated virtues of our time. We have all heard stories of mediocre athletes becoming outstanding, people with average talent succeeding, and those with normal abilities accomplishing the spectacular—all because of this thing called courage. Courage is life's great intangible, the invisible determinant, the great multiplying factor.

Scott Harris, Summit Expedition's former director, would take on King Kong blindfolded. Recently I discovered the source of many of his attitudes about life. He showed me something his father had written twenty years ago. It's well worth pondering: "Life is a journey," said C. R. Harris. "If I find myself, if I discover what I can be counted upon to do, the limits of my courage, the extent of my dedication, my ability to surrender part of my life to someone, my love of work and beauty, my goals, and the point from which I will no longer retreat—once I have these things, then I will have a mansion which I can occupy with dignity and respect all the years of my life. And this knowledge will truly make every day the best day of my life."

The Bible is a book jammed with courage—some examples are subtle, some are bold. In Deuteronomy 30, God challenges the Israelites to "choose life." In the next chapter, he says, three times, "Be strong and of *good* courage." And then a few pages later, in Joshua 1, he uses the same phrase—"Be strong and of *good* courage"—four more times.

Courage is such a vital element for the Christian that faith without courage is mere idealism. A courage-lacking faith will risk nothing. It won't go the extra step or even the extra minute.

Some years ago I came across this story of an incident that apparently took place in 1932 which speaks of the centrality of risk and courage in one's faith:

A man was walking across the desert, stumbling, almost dying of thirst, when he saw a well. As he approached the well, he found a note in a can close by. The note read: "Dear friend, there is enough water in this well, enough for all, but sometimes the leather washer gets dried up and you have to prime the pump. Now if you look underneath the rock just west of the well, you will find a bottle full of water, corked. Please don't drink the water. What you've got to do is take the bottle of water and pour the first half very slowly into the well to loosen up the leather washer. Then pour the rest in very fast and pump like crazy! You *will* get water. The well has never run dry. Have faith. And when you're done, don't forget to put the note back, fill up the bottle and put it back under the rock. Good luck. Have a fun trip. Sincerely, your friend, Desert Pete."

What would you do? You're on the verge of expiring from lack of water, and in reality, the bottle of water is only enough to quench your thirst, not save your life. Would you have the courage to risk it all?

This story is a powerful allegory about some of the essential ingredients in the Christian faith. First, there is *evidence* — there is a written message, the can with the letter in it, the bottle underneath the rock. Everything is in order, but there is no proof that you can really *trust* Desert Pete. The second element is *risk*. Here is a man dying of thirst asked to pour the only water he is sure of down the well. Faith is always costly. The third element is *work*. Some people have mistakenly interpreted faith as a substitute for work. Faith is not laziness. Desert Pete reminds us that after we trust and risk we must pump like crazy!

Jesus asks us to take our puny bottle of water and pour it in the well with guided instructions and then work real hard. He promises us not only enough to quench our thirst, but enough to quench the next person's thirst as well.

Another story is an old one you may have heard, but it's good enough to bear repeating. We use it, along with the Desert Pete story, in our Summit Expedition manual and in our courses to demonstrate the core of courage—its relationship with faith:

Once there was a tightrope walker who performed unbelievable aerial feats. All over Paris, he had done tightrope acts at great heights. He followed his initial acts with succeeding ones, walking blindfolded on the tightrope, and then doing that while pushing a wheelbarrow. A promoter in America heard about this and wrote him, inviting the daredevil to perform his act over the waters and dangers of Niagara Falls. He added, "I don't believe you can do it." The tightrope walker accepted the challenge.

After much promotion and planning, the man appeared before a huge crowd gathered to see the event. He was to start on the Canadian side and walk to the American side. Drums rolled and everyone gasped as they watched the performer walk across the wire blindfolded with a wheelbarrow. When he stepped off on the American side, the crowd went wild. Then the tightrope walker turned to the promoter and said, "Well, now do you believe I can do it?"

"Sure I do," the promoter answered. "I just saw you do it."

"No, no, no," said the tightrope walker. "Do you really believe I can do it?"

"I just said I did."

"I mean do you *really* believe?"

"Yes, I believe!"

"Good," said the tightrope walker, "then get in the wheelbarrow and we'll go back to the other side."

The word *believe* in Greek means "to live by." How often do we say that we believe Christ can do what he says, but we don't have the courage to get in the wheelbarrow? Our faith is not complete until it is accompanied by action.

It's interesting that the word *courage* comes from the old French root *corage*, meaning heart. We can know God primarily—though, of course not solely—with our hearts. Like the heart, courage pumps life into all the other virtues. However, what is "good" courage? It seems to be courage for the sake of others—active compassion. People who know God with their hearts have the courage to transform their convictions into energy and action for others' sake. People who don't are like cars without motors—they look great in the driveway, but they haven't got what it takes to get anybody anywhere. They look nice, but lack depth of character; they lack heart, the courage to translate the kingdom of niceness into the kingdom of God.

Where does this stuff come from, this big-heart courage? It comes from the inside out. We know that. It's sometimes called "extended effort," "bravery," "valor." In the street, it's known as "moxie." I tend to favor the word *guts*. In fact, in the front of one of my New Testaments there is an oversized magazine clipping that says simply: "I ADMIRE GUTS!" I do. I admire it in any size, shape, or form. I've seen it expressed in every possible living situation. On our Summit courses, I've seen it magnified many times over.

What does it look like? For some people, courage may be just being able to shake hands with the stranger next to them. Sometimes it could be just getting out of bed in the morning. Often it is the guts to stand up for one's beliefs. Sometimes it's the guts to change careers, to stretch one's limits, to begin a new lifestyle, to simplify, focus, and get involved with life on a deeper level. Often, it is the courage to doubt or to ask hard questions.

All of us can think of people we know who have this sort of gutsy courage. John Glenn, the famous astronaut, was once asked who was the most courageous person he'd ever known. Traveling in the circles he had, people speculated which famous person he'd pick—but they were to be surprised. His answer was stunning: "The most courageous person I know is my wife," he said without hesitation, "because she's demonstrated great courage by overcoming a speech impediment at the age of 46."

When I think of courage, I think of a friend named Sharon Taylor who is seriously handicapped and who struggles against great odds yet cheerfully works nights as a telephone operator, continuing to do wonderful things for so many others.

I think of Julie Kelley who has scaled a mountain in her wheelchair on our Go For It Program (our expedition for the physically disabled), who daily experiences the trials of spinal bifida, but who can light up a room with her innocent, genuine smile and her belief that she can do anything others can do.

And I think of Janet who demonstrated the quality of putting courage to work. The rappelling on one of our Summit courses frightened her. She was "petrified" with fear, having tried six times in vain. Finally, as we were just about to take down the equipment, assuring her she did not have to prove anything, she shook her head. She said, "No, this is to prove that Jesus Christ is *real* in my life," and she backed off the cliff and down the ropes.

When I think of the kind of gutsy courage that triumphs

despite the odds, I'm reminded of a friend named Tim Burton. I have mentioned my own fall earlier—it was a climbing accident, and I fell the equivalent of five stories. Although I am in constant pain, I still have all my mobility. Tim Burton was not so fortunate. He fell a mere eight feet, crushed his cerebellum and lost all his powers of equilibrium and much of his ability to speak. This big, strong man now lives in a wheelchair because he has no sense of balance whatsoever. Yet Tim is one of the most exciting people I have ever met.

I first met Tim on one of our Go For It courses. I can still see him now. The instructors were acting as living crutches for this bear of a man, one on either side of him. Yet he had so little balance and was so strong that he was throwing these instructors all over the mountain. Tim's enthusiasm was so absolutely unbridled as to be contagious. On one climb, he was so excited that all the way up he kept yelling "O H W-O-W!" in the methodical way he had learned to speak. "O H W-O-W! O H, W-O-W!" He said it so many times that we finally named the climb "Oh Wow!" in his honor.

I wake up to pain every morning, but the next day after Tim's "Oh Wow!" climb I wakened with pain of such terrible proportions that I could barely sit up. I confess that I was feeling sorry for myself, grumbling, "Lord, why, why? Give me a break!" I've begun to notice that whenever God catches me feeling sorry for myself, in his infinite wisdom and humor he will give me a living reminder of courage. That morning my living reminder was Tim Burton.

In the midst of my grumbling, I looked over and noticed that Tim, who'd been sleeping on the pad next to mine, was waking up. It took him almost thirty minutes to crawl out of his bag and finally turn over, propped on all fours. And he struggled without any complaints the whole time. As I watched the heroic courage of this young man, (and began feeling very embarrassed by my own grumblings and mumblings) Tim looked over and saw me. His face lit up and he said, in his slow, methodic way, "T i m! H o w a r e y o u? I a m r e a d y f o r a n y t h i n g!" It was his motto for life, he had told us. And I thought, O *Lord, you do still have much to teach us!*

Courage may come in strange packages. Have you ever thought that it might take guts to be still? Really still? That is almost unimaginable in this fast-lane world. But without stillness we'll never know our true spiritual selves. "Be still and know that I am God," the Scriptures say. Author and pastor Eugene Peterson has had the courage to take "stillness" seriously. He has decided to live out the Scriptures' sabbath principle which most of us take so lightly. The word *sabbath*, he explains, means "to quit," to cease striving, to rest in God. So he and his wife take one day a week to be still. They do nothing in the way of "work," nothing "utilitarian." They read, talk, take hikes, rest, and write letters to friends. He says this has reenergized his world and changed his ministry. He recommends that all of us can cut out half of what we do so we can do the other half well.

We all could make lists of such gutsy people. And sometimes it's good to look closely at courage in others for it helps us understand where courage comes from. Then we see how many areas of life it influences and how pervasive courage is in the lives of people all around us who are accomplishing worthwhile things.

In order for us to have such courage, though, we need one more intangible quality—*self-esteem*. The courage to *be* ourselves. We need a good, healthy dose of self-affirmation, in spite of the circumstances; or better yet, we need genuine God-affirmation.

The *multiplying factor* in a peak performance lifestyle is this healthy self-esteem. People with that are the ones who perform profoundly well. Courage then becomes easier. We must have a good amount of healthy self-affirmation before we can be the unique person we're created to be—in spite of the degree of difficulty of life, and in spite of the world that's screaming in our ears, "You don't measure up!"

When asked what was the greatest commandment of all,

Jesus said, "You shall love the Lord your God with all your heart, and with all your soul, and with all your mind. . . . you shall love your neighbor as yourself." Bruce Larson once interpreted that in a way I've never forgotten. He said, "That means to love God totally, love others unconditionally, and love ourselves *scandalously.*" One of the things we need to remember constantly is that we can love other people only in direct proportion to the way we love ourselves.

In the memorable play, *A Thousand Clowns*, Murray, a temporarily unemployed rebel against conventional society, has care of his twelve-year-old nephew. A social worker comes to discuss taking the boy out of Murray's care on grounds he is an unfit guardian. But Murray is worried about the boy's future:

> I just want him to stay with me till I can be sure he won't turn into a Norman Nothing. . . . [one of those nice dead people] I want him to be sure he'll know when he's chickening out on himself. I want him to get to know exactly the special thing he is or else he won't notice it when it starts to go. I want him to stay awake and know who the phonies are. . . . I want a little guts to show before I can let him go. I want to be sure he sees all the wild possibilities. I want him to know it's worth all the trouble just to give the world a little goosing when you get the chance. And I want him to know that subtle, sneaky, important reason why he was born a human being and not a chair.[10]

Healthy self-esteem is not optional. But our need for self-esteem is not only because of what it can do for us individually. One of the most important reasons we have to acquire the courage to be who we are and the courage to love ourselves in spite of all the negative we see, is because such God-confidence sets us *free* to love the world. Doing that, as we'll discuss later, is an integral part of the peak performance process.

I'd like to suggest seven ways to help you develop and exhibit this important element of courage, so you'll be free to live your life fully.

1. *You are the first, the best, and the only YOU that has ever been created.* Remember that. Think about that. There will never be another you. To understand your uniqueness is to celebrate it.

2. *You don't have to compare yourself with others.* We live in a society that pressures us by the hour, the minute, the second, to compare—and then in subtle (and not-so-subtle) ways tells us we don't measure up. But I say when you compare, you lose. Believing you are not as good as someone else is wasted time and a false assumption.

But believing you're better than someone else is also wrong, especially in terms of the kingdom's values. Even comparing in order to declare that you're equal with another is a misunderstanding. We all have equal opportunities, but according to our kingdom value system, each is absolutely unique.

3. *You are not your actions.* Keep this fact in mind, always.

One of the most important things I can do as a father is to separate my kids' personhood from their behavior. If I do, I have the opportunity to love them unconditionally even though I get frustrated at times with some of the things they do. I may not like what they do, but I can still love who they are.

The same goes for myself. I may not like what I do. I may need to ask forgiveness ten times a day. I may want to heap guilt on my head and talk myself into hating myself. But if I realize that my personhood is uniquely worthwhile—that God loves the sinner, but not the sin—then I can see myself as worthwhile no matter what my actions are.

4. *Employ solid decision-making.* Self-acceptance is a courageous act of decision. This point is critical. At some moment in time, you've got to draw that mental line and take that step over it, saying, "I accept myself unconditionally." No one can figure out your worth but you. If someone else could give you self-acceptance, they'd call it "other acceptance."

Why should you do this? The main reason is that *any* other option is lousy; any other option doesn't make sense. Too many people burn up great amounts of energy wavering back and forth as to whether or not they are going to accept themselves. And they lose years which could be spent in giving to themselves and to others. The decision is solid. It's time to make it firmly.

5. *Allow yourself to make mistakes.* Remember that mistakes are the stepping stones to achievement. As we'll discuss later, failure can be a positive word, as crazy as that sounds. In fact, it can be one of the greatest teachers life offers.

Bob Moward, who created many of the concepts here, does a mental exercise that we would do well to emulate. He gives himself five mistakes every day. The first five are free. "They're on the house," he explains. "And if I only make four mistakes today, I get six the next day." It's his way of reminding himself that mistakes are normal and can actually be stepping stones to success.

6. *Enjoy each day, one at a time.* We are called to live in the present. A person can live in three tenses—past, present, and future. We can spend so much of our time and energy feeling guilty over the past and worrying about the future that there's not much time to enjoy the present.

A friend of mine got his words mixed up one day and said, "All we have is the past, the *pleasant,* and the future." I like that. We are called to live in the "pleasant" tense. We are called to live each day, one minute, one second at a time. And to enjoy them to the fullest.

7. *Give yourself plenty of praise and encouragement.* Why? Because you are doing a terrific job. Surprised? You shouldn't be. Whether you believe it or not, that is exactly what you're doing. Being a human being is so difficult and complex that for you to have come this far means you are doing wonderfully. So you should give yourself plenty of praise and encouragement.

Have you ever noticed your own "self-talk"? When we speak normally, we do so at the rate of about 120 words a minute. But psychologists have helped us understand also about our self-talk. When we talk to ourselves, we do so at a rate of about *thirteen hundred words a minute!* And the bad news is that 70 percent or so of our self-talk normally is negative. That means that you and I spend quite a bit of time saying such things as *Oh no, I shouldn't have done that,* or *Oh, what a jerk I am,* and other similar, self-defeating phrases.

If you could change your self-talk tone, I guarantee that would change your whole outlook. If you were to suddenly begin to give yourself affirmation, saying, for instance, *Now, that's more like me, that's more the way I want to be,* just think how you would begin to see yourself! If you change your words you can change your image and, in turn, change your behavior.

Accept yourself. God wants all of you, not just the good parts of you. God doesn't love you because you are good, but because you're a special, unique, one-of-a-kind human being. "Just to be is a blessing," says Abraham Heschel. "Just to live is holy." Have the courage to accept yourself fully, so you can be freed to become the very best you can be—and live a whole and holy life.

> To be nobody but yourself
> in a world which is doing
> its best night and day
> to make you everybody else—
> means to fight the hardest battle
> which any human being can fight—
> —and never stop fighting.
> —e.e. cummings

10
Teamwork

I am more than I am, but less than we are.

> I sought my God
>> but my God I could not see.
> I sought my soul,
>> but my soul eluded me.
> I sought my brother,
>> and I found all three.
>> *—author unknown*

For where two or three are gathered in my name, there am I in the midst of them.   —Matthew 18:20

There's a wonderful story about Jimmy Durante, one of the great entertainers of a generation ago. He was asked to be a part of a show for World War II veterans. He told them his schedule was very busy and he could afford only a few minutes, but if they wouldn't mind his doing one short monologue and immediately leaving for his next appointment, he would come. Of course, the show's director agreed happily.

But when Jimmy got on stage, something interesting happened. He went through the short monologue and then stayed. The applause grew louder and louder and he kept staying. Pretty soon, he had been on fifteen, twenty, then thirty minutes. Finally he took a last bow and left the stage. Backstage someone stopped him and said, "I thought you had to go after a few minutes. What happened?"

Jimmy answered, "I did have to go, but I can show you the

reason I stayed. You can see for yourself if you'll look down on the front row." In the front row were two men, each of whom had lost an arm in the war. One had lost his right arm and the other had lost his left. Together, they were able to clap, and that's exactly what they were doing, loudly and cheerfully.

That's teamwork, in action and in spirit. What does team-work have to do with our peak performance lifestyle? As we've said, ours is not the normal concept of peak performance. Our process of becoming "whole" cannot exist without others. As the poet W. H. Auden has said so boldly: "We must love one another or die." Our lifestyle must be unself-consciously *with* and *toward* others.

We really do need each other, and we need to work with one another. In the opening pages of Scripture God looked upon the culmination of his creation and said: "It is not good for man to be alone." Later, when Jesus offered criteria for how the world would know his disciples, he gave only two—"by bear-ing much fruit" (the peak performance process?) and by obey-ing his new commandment, "loving each other . . . *even as he has loved us*" (John 15:8; 13:34). Teamwork is what makes that love possible, tangible. It wasn't in vain that Christ said, "Where two or three are gathered together, there I am in their midst." Our working together is important, vital to him. There is an "*us*-ness" to the Christian faith.

And when teamwork is working well, there's a potent magic about it. That's when it's "synergy." The word *synergy* means that "the sum total is greater than the total of the separate parts." Stemming from the roots "syn" and "ergo" (meaning "to work together") it implies that a team can be far more powerful than the separate members working individually. For instance, it is estimated that if I could get all the muscles in my body to pull in one direction—I could lift over twenty-five tons.

The great thinker Buckminster Fuller in his book *Synergetics* explains that it is very possible that "one plus one can equal four if we put our efforts together in the same direction." I believe that God designed it that way, and designed us to need each other in that way.

In John 17, Jesus says "may they be one *even as we are one*" (italics mine), and he repeats the essence of the phrase at least five times in one chapter. That gives us a strong indication of how important the message is for us. We are called to be the body of Christ. The word *community* comes from the same word as communion and communication. Communion, we must remember, is made up of broken bread and crushed grapes. So, it is in our brokenness and our imperfections, that we are called to come together and help each other be whole— the best we can be.

The fact that we are called the "body" of Christ is very integral to this idea, too. Physiologically, every cell in the body is designed for every other cell. The whole purpose of each cell is to enable all the other cells to perform. The only cell that exists for itself is a cancer cell.

Although the peak performance process is a personal pilgrimage, it does not require that we be "rugged individualists." The image of the all-American who pulls himself up by his own bootstraps, is a totally foreign one to the Christian faith, and likewise, then, to the process of peak performance. We're just not built that way, no matter what our world is shouting. We need each other, and when we work with each other, great things happen.

When I think of teamwork, I think of the Go For It Program of our Summit Expedition ministry. If you recall, this is a remarkable course we run for handicapped participants. And it is based on teamwork. For every disabled student there is one able-bodied person and one instructor. The able-bodied person is called a TAB, a "temporarily able-body." Teamwork is definitely the heartbeat of the course. It would never work if it weren't for the eloquent, exquisite, and persistent teamwork.

To take a wheelchair up the mountain, we normally have to put people behind the wheelchair, tie slings under the front of the wheelchair, and have the TABs work as horses pulling the wheelchair up. When we go cross-country, there are places where we literally have to lift the chairs up and carry the student and the chair across. Sometimes we have to be creative. For instance, sometimes the TABs are living crutches or act as the eyes of a blind student, leading the student up the mountain. We've taken every kind of disabled person on these courses.

You'd think it would be hard to line up instructors for this course. But every year we have a waiting list for what these young people call the "privilege" of serving as a TAB because the disabled students give so much back. Courage, compassion, perseverance—it takes all those from the students and the TAB instructors. The love is so literally palatable and tangible you can taste it. And teamwork is the magic that makes it happen.

Not to understand this about teamwork is not to understand why God instituted the church.

Someone flippantly said,

Christians don't dance.

Christians don't drink.

Christians don't swear.

Christians don't smoke . . . and

Christians don't like each other.

We all know there is more truth in that little ditty than we care to admit. We don't seem to get along very well, so the power of teamwork is lost on many, many Christians. But the spirit of teamwork and community comes from a sacrificial, unconditional love we are meant to have for each other.

At the end of many of our Summit Expedition courses, we have a final "agape celebration" in which we sing and enjoy a time of skits and worship and sharing. Old, young, handicapped, every sort of student has a great time. We conclude the celebration with the Lord's Supper, followed by a service of foot washing.

These are feet that have been wearing boots all week, weary feet that have been in constant use in the wilderness. As a demonstration of the quality of love and teamwork that has grown among us, we participate in this ritual joyfully. We remove each other's boots and socks that smell just like you think they would, then—with water and a cloth—one washes the other's feet and shares how much that person meant to him or her during the course. We virtually thank one another for the privilege of letting us serve each other. All of us see it as a wonderful symbol for the course and for the servant-leader lifestyle we want to take home with us. Amidst smiles and laughter, this service is a real-life celebration of the servant nature of Christ, in whose nature we can participate.

But we are all so different. Is it possible to work together, to get along so well that we "synergize"? At a seminar I attended over twenty years ago, the speaker said something so true I remember it today. He said, "There is only one thing we know for sure about conflict—and that is it's inevitable." Yes, it is inevitable, but it can also be vital. Conflict doesn't necessarily have to be negative. Like different notes on a piano keyboard, the differences can be made into something harmonious if a little effort is involved. In fact, if we didn't have differences— we wouldn't have music.

Some years ago I had the privilege of being called in to help arbitrate some severe difficulties and conflicts that had emerged among inner-city workers for a large Christian organization. The arguments were intense. Voices were raised. The issues were complex and very heated. After hours of vented anger and frustration, some—but not all—of the problems began to be resolved. When we finished there were still problems to be solved and feelings to be assuaged—but I'll never forget the prayer by a young woman who had only hours before been right in the middle of the hottest arguing. She said, with her voice cracking, "Lord, I want to thank you for putting each person in this room in my life . . . so that I can be more like your Son."

Teamwork is not an option. The world will know Christ's followers primarily by how they love one another. That love is crucial to effective teamwork.

Dietrich Bonhoeffer wrote a classic book on community called *Life Together*. In it he reminds us that "Christian community is simply and solely what Jesus Christ has done for you and done for me." That's the only criterion. "For Jesus Christ alone is our unity. He is our peace. Through him alone do we have access to one another, joy in one another, and fellowship with one another." The problem, says Bonhoeffer, oftentimes, is we try to "build" community rather than accept it. It is not an ideal which we must strive to realize and develop; it is rather a reality created by God, given through Christ, in which we may participate. "Innumerable times a whole Christian community has broken down because it sprung from a wish-dream. The serious Christian, set down for the first time in a Christian community, is likely to bring with him a very definite idea of what Christian life together should be and try to realize it. But God's grace speedily shatters such dreams. Just as surely as God desires to lead us to a knowledge of genuine Christian fellowship, so surely must we be overwhelmed by a great disillusionment with others, with Christians in general, and if we are fortunate, with ourselves."

We are a team because of what Jesus has done for us, and by the fact that we've accepted him as our Lord. So what remains for us is to learn how to love each other . . . as Christ loves us.

Our tendency, though, is to want to build the right sort of fellowship, to try to create *good* Christian community in order to honor God. We have good intentions ("wish-dreams"). But these get in the way of genuinely accepting each other and truly working together. He states that the sooner God crushes our "wish-dreams of community" and gets us to the reality of Jesus Christ, the better off we are. Community is a divine reality, not a Christian ideal. We don't build it; we accept it the way it is. And when we do that, we get on with experiencing the power of teamwork—and the excitement of it.

There's no way to be fully human alone. We need each other—to laugh, to cry, to listen, to challenge, and to encourage each other. Christianity is something lived in context. In fact, in 1 Corinthians, when Paul wrote "you are the temple of the Holy Spirit," it is significant to note that the word "you" is plural. Together we are the temple of the Holy Spirit. There truly is an "us-ness" to the faith. It is us together who will bring glory to God.

Suppose, at the end of my life, the Enemy were to hold me up by one foot in front of God, waggle me a little, and with a sneer on his face, say, "This ol' Hansel character proves that your plan didn't work. Look at the lousy job he did of living out the Christian life." And then suppose he spends hours listing my sins. After three volumes full, he takes a breath and sneers, "and that was only for last November." But God intervenes. Shaking his mighty head, he says, "No, you don't understand my plan. That's not the purpose. The purpose was not for Tim Hansel to live out the whole Christian faith by himself. If you want to play this little game, then you have to hold up the entire body of Christ. And when you see the entire body of Christians, you will see that every temptation was withstood and every accomplishment has been completed and everything I ever planned has been fulfilled—through the body of Christ, not through any single individual!"

That story has given me great freedom to realize that I am only called to live out my share of the Christian faith, to play my part in the body of Christ. I am not alone.

Don't try to go it alone. The Holy Sweat process of peak performance entails a firm fix on others, and a firm understanding of how we need each other and how the power of teamwork multiplies as we work together.

11
A Passion for Excellence

The quality of a person's life is in direct proportion to his commitment to excellence, regardless of his chosen field of endeavor. —*Vincent T. Lombardi*

Genius is one percent inspiration and ninety-nine percent perspiration. —*Thomas Alva Edison*

Excellence is to do a common thing in an uncommon way. —*Booker T. Washington*

Do you ever wonder how good, *really* good you could be at something? What area is it you're thinking of? It might be a hobby, or your job, or a talent or a sport you love. It might even be a certain type of person you'd like to be. Whatever it is, does it ever cross your mind that you probably could be a lot better at that than you are right now?

You know what I mean. Maybe the little longing is brought on by seeing someone else excel in your particular area of interest. Every once in a while, you get that little twinge . . . and you wonder what would happen if you would just give a little more to it, set your sights a little higher. Would you excel too?

Well, what do you need to get you going? Whether you're aware of it or not, your mind knows your innate need for excellence and is continually offering you that very challenge. Deep down, you've understood that need for challenge ever since you were a kid, when one "I dare you!" could get your pulses pumping and your juices flowing.

Think back to those disciples who chose to follow Jesus. Think about what Jesus offered them. Take up your cross and follow me, shake the dust from your feet, have no roof over your heads, be persecuted, find the way narrow and rough, leave family and friends . . . follow me, and I'll make you fishers of men!

Why would anyone want to join such a group? Because those rare men not only loved a challenge, but they had a fiery *passion for excellence*. They knew a life of ease and comfort was not a true life goal and would give no lasting fulfillment.

Alan Loy McGinnis says in *Bringing Out the Best in People*,

> It is a canard of our culture that we would be happier if we weren't so busy, if we weren't working so hard, if we didn't have so much homework. If only we could relax more and take more vacations. But . . . the happiest people have found some cause and they stride through life propelled by a commitment. The fact of the matter is that most people are bored.[11]

Whether we accept the challenge our minds are continually presenting to us or not, we all need a commitment, a challenge to excel. Otherwise, we are, more than not, quite bored. Most people feel a need to be good at something.

We are talking here about a *passion* for excellence. The term, if you think about it, is another oxymoron, a paradox. Excellence seems so tightly controlled, passion so unbridled, wild, exuberant. But the reason I've coined the term in just this way is that the two concepts need each other to become real. We have that tug toward excellence. Our minds challenge us to do our very best. But without some healthy passion behind that desire, we will never actually begin such a quest for our best.

And what is our most excellent self? We all need to pick our own areas of excellence and then simply strive to be our very best—stretching, risking, hoping, enduring. That's part of the process of the peak performance lifestyle. But ultimately, *we* are the only ones who can measure the quality of our own excellence. "If a man is called to be a street sweeper," Martin Luther King, Jr., once said, "he should sweep streets even as Michelangelo painted, or as Beethoven composed music or as Shakespeare wrote poetry. He should sweep streets so that all the hosts of heaven and earth will pause to say, 'Here lived a great street sweeper who did his job well.'"

I think we also have to understand our own *innate* excellence before we can reach for the best we have to give. We as human beings are living miracles. We are, as the psalmist says, "fearfully and wonderfully made." I don't know if you realize it, but you and I produce about three billion red blood cells every day, about a million a minute. I told that to a group one time and then asked, "How does that make you feel?" I expected them to be astonished and excited. One guy said, "Tired." We all laughed. But we *should* be appropriately awestruck, actually. We've got approximately sixty thousand miles of capillaries running through our bodies. In some places, the cells have to line up one by one to go through in order to do what they are supposed to do. And this is all choreographed without the least bit of conscious thought on our part.

The human eye can see an estimated 8 *million* different colors. It's also estimated that 2 million signals are hitting our nervous system every second. We are Nature's greatest miracle. Our brain is capable of making and storing enough connections and information that the total number would be expressed by a one followed by 6.5 million miles of zeros—a number that would stretch between the earth and moon and back fourteen times.

We could go on and on. "Fearfully and wonderfully made" begins to take on a whole new meaning. And our attitude of gratitude should be a little more acute, as, hopefully, we begin to realize what special beings we are and what special people we can become.

When I speak of personal excellence I don't mean "average today, outstanding tomorrow." There aren't any quantum leaps in excellence. Excellence is realized inch by inch. It begins as an attitude, and soon the passion pushes it into all areas of our lives, big and small. In fact, excellence must begin in the little areas or else the big areas will never be touched.

In their book about business excellence, entitled *A Passion for Excellence,* Tom Peters and Nancy Austin explain an important principle that can pertain to us, too. In business, they say, excellence is decided by the way a secretary answers you on the phone, by the way the clerk handles your package, by the way some people—who may seem unimportant in the whole scheme of the company—treat you as a customer. The authors keep implying all through the book that it is excellence in small things, in the minor details, that makes a picture of excellence for the whole company.

I've been most impressed by people who have sought quality and excellence in the subtle areas of their lives—in kindness and courtesy, for instance. Frederick Buechner has said, if you want to be holy, be *kind.* For most people, excellence is easiest sought and found first in little areas. In physical fitness, for instance, excellence comes in subtle things—how we eat, how we treat our body, the consistency of our exercise. That's why we hear, "train, don't strain." Your body changes slowly as you pay attention to such subtle things. And so it is with the other areas of our lives.

A passion for excellence, then, is manifested most in small ways: a mom who cooks her family a delightful meal; a dad who stops work to "kidnap" his family for a day; a student who does his best on a small quiz; a gymnast who stretches for that extra millimeter; a business person who treats customers and colleagues in the same excellent fashion; that fourth-grade Sunday school teacher who does extra work to make the lesson come alive; the coach who does minute things to help his or her young athletes not only be better athletes but better young people; that church member who attends church to truly worship, to listen as if being there was for allowing God to change his or her life. When we pay attention to a small area of excellence, we are giving ourselves realistic goals to excel in, and those experiences will propel us forward.

Are there any restrictions to this passion for excellence? Can we be too old or too young? Can our physical or mental limitations keep us from excelling? Not a bit. Anyone can be a peak performer in this lifestyle process, because, remember—we are striving for excellence within ourselves. That's the essential that counts. *Our* best.

Three friends of mine prove that point. Jim Milhon, football coach at Azusa Pacific University, celebrated his fiftieth birthday by biking across the United States. Orv Mestad, 63, is just beginning to hit his stride. In the past two years, he's climbed mountains in Alaska, scaled the eastern face of Mount Whitney, and taken a group of young people to Ghana during the summer. And I have to admit, I can hardly keep up with him on a bike.

Greg Fisher demonstrates an unbelievable passion for excellence. And more than that, he reminds me that sometimes our restrictions are mainly self-imposed or imposed by the opinions of others. Greg was part of our Go For It Expedition some years ago. He has two artificial legs and one full arm, with only three fingers. The other arm is only partially formed.

He said to me one day, "I want to talk to Gaffney about weight lifting." Tim Gaffney, one of our instructors, is a fine weight lifter. Mentally trying to picture this young man with those big weights, I said to Greg, "You want to get into weight lifting?" "No," he said, "I just want to get better." He seemed so determined, with this fierce look in his eyes. So I asked, "What events can you do?" "My best is the bench press," he said. Even with his artificial legs he weighed less than 150 pounds.

Then I said something I wished I could have taken back the moment it came from my lips. I asked, "What's your best?" I wanted to hide my head, thinking what an embarrassing question to ask this young man so seriously handicapped. But I'm glad I did, for his answer was unforgettable:

"My best is 325, *but I know I can do better.*"

I was delightfully stunned. At the peak of my athletic career, I once lifted three hundred pounds, and I felt like I had the continents of Asia on one side and Europe on the other. Greg helped me realize again how seriously we all tend to underestimate ourselves.

Are you really giving life your best shot? Are you going after your days as if they really count? I'd rather make my days count than simply count my days. The key is to go for excellence in small segments. Ask yourself, what can I do in the next hour that would somehow improve the quality of my life or someone's around me.

I see excellence in a person's trying to learn how to read a little faster. I see excellence in spending ten more minutes in Bible study or private devotions. I see excellence in the quiet things done for others—such as the friend who recently told me, "I just want you to know that as of Friday, I will have prayed for you every day for five years." I see excellence in commitment and compassion.

Perhaps we can keep in mind the type of selfless excellence C. S. Lewis believed in. He once likened his role as a Christian writer to an adjective striving to point others to the Noun of Truth. For people to believe that Noun, we must polish our adjectives. In whatever segment of life we choose to funnel our passion for excellence, we can find an even deeper passion in realizing that we are simply serving the Noun in the best way we can.

12
The Ability to Fail

If you want to double your success rate, double your failure rate.
—*Thomas Watson*
president, IBM

Success is never final. Failure is never fatal. It is courage that counts.
—*Winston Churchill*

He who has never failed somewhere, that man cannot be great. Failure is the true test of greatness.
—*F. D. Mattiesen*

A young man had just been elected to take over as bank president. He strode into the outgoing bank president's office and said, "Sir, I would like your advice. What will make me as successful as you?"

The older man looked up from his papers, eyed the young man up and down and rather curtly said, "Two words: Good decisions!"

The young man thanked the outgoing president and left the office. But then he turned and knocked on the door and said, "Please forgive me for bothering you again, but how does a person know he's making good decisions?"

The bank president waited for a moment. Then, going back to his work, he said, "One word: Experience!"

The young man nodded, and turned to walk out. But before he reached the door, he stopped and turned around.

"Yes?" said the outgoing president, putting the papers down again.

"Well," the young man asked, "how do I get that experience?"

"Two words," the other man answered. "Bad decisions!"

Bad decisions. Mistakes. *Failure.* We don't like to admit it, but we know the terms well.

Including failure in the discussion of peak performance keys may seem unusual, yet, believe it or not, the ability to fail successfully is one of the most critical ingredients of living a lifestyle at our peak level. Failure may be the taproot of our relationship with Jesus Christ. To become Christians, we have to admit we are failures. We can't make it on our own. We must admit to failure to gain an entrance exam into the kingdom. How about *that* for failing successfully?

Yet sometimes our need, our drive for success keeps us from understanding the true nature and purpose of failure. We are not talking about just failing. We are talking about allowing ourselves *the freedom to fail.*

NASA experts know that their vehicles in space always need adjusting. In fact, as I understand it, they are never on target. The most critical aspect is what the experts call the "attitude" of the vehicle. So it is with the process of becoming your very best. Life is made up of thousands of failures. How then does anyone succeed? The secret is: *attitude.* Failures are only temporary set-backs at worst, and bits of wisdom at best—when your attitude is right. Such an attitude coupled with the willingness to fail are essential.

In the process of inventing the light bulb, I understand that Thomas Edison failed almost eight thousand times before he got it right. That's burning a lot of midnight oil. When asked how he felt about all that failure, the great genius replied simply: "They weren't failures," he said. "They were education." There is no better education than your own failures, if you've the eyes to see. We must have the courage to fail. It's evidence that we're risking to be our best.

There is a true story about a project manager at IBM who lost the company 10 million dollars. Dejectedly, he walked into the president's office and said, "I'm sorry. I'm sure you'll want my resignation. I'll be gone by the end of the day."

The president's response showed his understanding of the value of failure. He said, "Are you kidding? We've just invested 10 million dollars in your education. We're not about to let you go. Now get back to work."

People who understand failure and success in their appropriate contexts are free to try anything. Summit Expedition sponsors an insane bike-a-thon called the Whitney Classic to raise money for a project involving handicapped and delinquent kids. We attempt to go from the lowest elevation of the continental United States at Badwater in Death Valley, California (282 feet below sea level), to the highest, Mount Whitney, (14,494 feet above sea level) in a twenty-four-hour period.

Recently, we filmed portions of the Classic in which forty-nine riders began. Of the forty-nine, only a handful made it to the top. Did the rest fail? I don't think so. They had set their own limits, stretched and learned about themselves, and enjoyed the freedom to try. In a real way, those of us who attempted it saw the ride as a metaphor of the peak performance lifestyle, so much so that we used those film highlights as the backbone of our Holy Sweat film series.

All the people who participated in that grueling ride excelled in their own way. And they knew it. That's the magic of the freedom to try and fail. But there are many who are so caught up with success and so worried about failing that they continue to live timid, cautious lives.

I love this parable about such safe, tidy living; it illustrates my point brilliantly:

> He saw people love each other. . . . And he saw that all love made strenuous demands on the lovers. He saw love require sacrifice and self-denial. He saw love produce arguments and anguish. . . . And he decided that it cost too much. And he decided not to diminish his life with love.
>
> He saw people strive for distant and hazy goals. He saw men strive for success . . . women strive for high, high,

ideals. . . . And he saw that the striving was frequently mixed with disappointment. And he saw the strong men fail. . . . He saw it force people into pettiness. . . . He saw that those who succeeded were sometimes those who had not earned the success. And he decided that it cost too much. He decided not to soil his life with striving.

He saw people serving others. He saw men give money to the poor and helpless. . . . And he saw that the more they served, the faster the need grew. . . . He saw ungrateful receivers turn on their serving friends. . . . He decided not to soil his life with serving.

And when he died, he walked up to God and presented him with his life. Undiminished, unmarred, and unsoiled, his life was clean from the filth of the world, and he presented it proudly . . . saying, "This is my life."

And the great God said, "What life?"[12]

What keeps us so cautious and afraid is our warped concept of success. Some people cannot act because they are so afraid of what might happen if they fail. They are constantly afraid of what others will think. Their concept of success is measured only by what they see and what they are told, not by what they are. But as someone wise once said, "I don't know what success is, but I know what failure is. *Failure is trying to please everybody.*"

"Success imprisons," Eugene Peterson puts it bluntly. "Success is an unbiblical burden stupidly assumed by prideful persons who reject the risks and perils of faith, preferring to appear right rather than to be human."

What we are talking about is freedom. It sounds strange, talking about freedom and failure in the same sentence, doesn't it? But they are unavoidably connected.

Do I mean that all people who fail are somehow free? No. But those who are free to fail while striving for excellence are the most free. The more we stretch for our best, the more we will fail. But the more we'll experience, too. "Fear of failure inhibits freedom; the freedom to fail encourages it," Peterson goes on to say. "The life of faith encourages the risk taking that frequently results in failure, for it encourages human ventures into crisis and the unknown."

Sometimes we are going to fall on our respective faces. These failures don't have to be cataclysmic endings. They can be the avenues down which we understand ourselves better and experience God's grace more widely and deeply.

As you begin the process of your peak performance lifestyle, you'll learn that failure is simply a part of it all. In striving, risking to be your best, you are almost virtually guaranteed to fail at some point. You still may not believe it, but that is actually good news.

Is it just a coincidence that the Bible is a rich tapestry of failure and faith? Psalm 23, that incredible statement of confidence and security, comes immediately after David's statement in Psalm 22 about how he had become scorned by man. In the midst of these awful feelings of failure David understood God's power, and then wrote the masterpiece of faith that touches us thousands of years later.

Failure gives us the freedom to change. We can no longer pretend to be self-sufficient and independent. We don't have to keep pretending that we're different from the rest of the human race. So it should be easy to admit our failures to others, right? Wrong. It is not easy. James 5:16 says we are healed in direct proportion to how much we confess to one another. We are encouraged to be in the habit of admitting our sins to each other and praying for each other. That's the way we are healed and become whole. The fact that we conceal our failures from one another almost made me give up on myself as a Christian.

My life includes a long list of failures. I've kidded with some people that I didn't even become a Christian in the "right" way. As I mentioned before, I'm one of those Christians who doesn't know the exact time and place or even the moment when I became a Christian. I struggled, doubted, and at times simply refused to allow God's grace to change me. My conversion was a long, drawn-out, difficult process that lasted over a period of years. I feel somewhat like C.S. Lewis who said he was dragged "kicking and screaming" into the kingdom.

When I first became a Christian, I found my wild behavior somewhat hard to break. My philosophy of life at that time would be best described as "somewhere to the left of Whoopee." I was having a very difficult time directing my life in a new direction. It was more than a little frustrating. What made it even worse was the fact that other Christians around me were either unable or unwilling to share their failures and struggles with me. Several Christians actually told me that Christians aren't supposed to fail. Everyone, it seemed, had the Christian life wired. I became convinced that I was the only one who didn't have his act together. I was wrestling with immense guilt. After about a year of struggle, I came to the conclusion that God couldn't love me. No matter how hard I tried, I was just too fouled up. I was convinced that I was defective in the kingdom.

Fortunately, a dear friend, Don McClean, leveled with me about some of his problems. He told me about the personal temptations and struggles he had been battling for years—and some of them were exactly like my own. As this deeply spiritual man was talking, I realized that if *he* had these struggles, then maybe I wasn't completely hopeless after all. His "confession," his honest sharing, totally changed my life. To this day, I thank Don with all my heart. In fact, my oldest son's middle name is McClean, in honor of this man who so changed my life with his honesty and compassion.

I'll never forget something that my college landlady said to me. I asked her, "Mrs. Dingler, if my 'old self' is crucified with Christ, why is it still wiggling?"

She gave me this gentle smile and said, "Tim, you've got to remember that crucifixion is a slow death."

To be a Christian means to struggle with failure. As Charles Colson explained in *Loving God*,

God doesn't want our success, he wants us. He doesn't demand achievements, he demands obedience. . . . For through the ugly defeat of the cross, a holy God is utterly glorified. Victory comes through defeat, healing comes through brokenness and finding one's self comes through losing one's self.[13]

The very nature of obedience is this: God calls us to give without regard to circumstances or results. In fact, Jesus himself never tried to save himself or to assure his own success. Why then should we?

An ambitious failure is better than no attempt at all. Failure gives us the freedom to change, without fear of what others think. In 1 Thessalonians 2:4, Paul explains, in effect, "You don't understand us, we come not to please men, but to please God."

I'm continually amazed with my own failures. But the wonder of it all is that God keeps working on me and through me anyway. I'm convinced he's worked more through my failures than my successes. I'm so grateful the Bible is packed with failures who became champions of the faith: the Peters, the Davids, the Moseses, the John Marks, and the Jonahs. Their stories show me that God isn't looking at our achievements, but at us—and that even my failures can be used for his ultimate glory.

My favorite failure is Peter. He spent three years at the Messiah's elbow, but when it came to a crisis, Peter denied him three times—two of those times were to little damsels. In that story, and in all of Peter's other failure stories, I am taught that we are called to the gospel of the second chance.

Think about the resurrection story as told in Mark 16. In verse 7, the angel tells Mary and the others to go tell the disciples—and who? The disciples *and Peter*. Those last two words are significant. It makes the whole statement remarkable. The one who had failed most miserably was named specifically so he would know he was forgiven and granted another chance. That was the moment that Peter was on his way to becoming "The Rock," the great leader he turned out to be.

The thief on the cross has always intrigued me, too. What was Christ trying to teach us? Here was a guy who had wasted his life and had done nothing to deserve grace. He had been nothing but a miserable failure. But Christ told him that the man would be with him in paradise. That statement reminds me in rich, sure strokes that God's love for us is so unconditional it overwhelms even our failures. That knowledge can give us all the strength and courage we need to risk—and to fail.

In *Bringing Out the Best in People*, Alan Loy McGinnis quotes a wise man who believes that "strong people make as many and as ghastly mistakes as weak people. The difference is that strong people admit them, laugh at them, learn from them. That is how they become strong."

Throughout history people have failed and failed and failed some more. I believe the difference in those who have led lives of excellence and those who have led lives of ultimate failure lies in their willingness to fail and learn from their failures. One famous man's life serves to illustrate this perhaps best of all:

1831   He failed in business.
1832   He was defeated in legislature.
1833   He again failed in business.
1834   He was elected to the legislature.
1835   His wife-to-be died.
1836   He had a nervous breakdown.
1838   He was defeated for Speaker of the House.
1840   He was defeated for Elector.
1850   A son died.
1855   He was defeated for the Senate.
1856   He was defeated for Vice-President.
1858   He was defeated for the Senate.
1860   This man, Abraham Lincoln, was elected President.[14]

Someone taught Lincoln that failure was not permanent, that failure was opportunity. And his strength grew.

We need to create environments where failure is not fatal. We need to give ourselves the freedom to fail. We aren't aiming at perfection, but at wholeness. We *can* learn how to handle rejection, and then we can help others handle it. The freedom to fail opens the door to a new wisdom and maturity. Only those who dare to fail greatly can ever achieve greatly.

13
Perseverance

To be able to fail well is absolutely critical. But the ability to make failure work *for* you and not *against* you requires one more quality: perseverance. This elusive characteristic is vital, because being able to fail means nothing if you don't have the ability to bounce back.

My near-fatal accident has taught me all I want to know—and I hope, all I need to know—about the importance of failure *plus* perseverance. The accident happened over a decade ago, in 1974, as I explain in the book *You Gotta Keep Dancin'*. I was with a friend, doing snow-, ice-, and rock-climbing on a splendid day. We had concluded a wonderful climb, and were almost back to the bottom. All we had to do was cross the snow bridge over one crevasse, which, as you know, is a huge opening in the ice where a glacier pulls apart. This one happened to be about five stories deep.

We were tired yet exuberant from our exhilarating climb. Neither of us had noticed that the surface of the snow over the crevasse had changed, causing the ordinarily firm footing to be slippery. Snow began balling up under my crampons (spikes attached to the bottom of a hiker's boots) until I suddenly slipped. In a flash, I slid down to the edge, flipped over upside down, and fell toward the bottom where I landed on the back of my neck.

It could have been worse. The ice pick around my wrist could have skewered me. And the large boulder at the bottom could have broken my neck. But it could have been a lot better, too. If I hadn't flipped over, my legs would have hit first instead of my upper body. If there had been anything between me and the bottom to break the fall, my impact wouldn't have been so devastating.

But when I came to, I surprised both my friend and myself by actually getting up, climbing out of the crevasse with him and hiking back to the base camp. Everything seemed okay as we returned home, until the shock wore off. And that's when the splitting, aching, agony of pain hit.

From that moment, my life has never been the same. After rounds and rounds of doctors and x-rays, I was told that I had fractured vertebrae and several crushed discs, and that there were bone fragments in my neck. I was lucky I wasn't a quadraplegic, they all said. I was indeed fortunate just to be alive.

But later, I was finally told that the pain would be permanent; it would be intense and chronic. That was the way it would be. So, as the struggles continued, I had to decide what power the pain would have over my life. I still had a choice, I realized. The choice wasn't as easy as some people imagine. And it continues to be a daily, sometimes hourly, choice to make. The lessons about perseverance come daily and hourly, too.

Perseverance is courage stretched out. One of the biblical words for it suggests that it is courage under pressure, under strenuous conditions. Since the writing of *You Gotta Keep Dancin'*, about my struggle to choose joy over pain, I've had people ask me if I am joyous all the time. Somehow many readers came to believe that in my choosing to persevere in as joyful a way as I can, my pain somehow vanished. Or if not that, I evidently had such strength of will that I overcame the pain to the extent that I now live in continual joy.

It's just not so. Our perception of joy needs to be adjusted, as we will discuss later. And as for my pain, it continues to be so difficult, so bad at times that many days it's hard just to function. Even the writing of this book has been slowed down numerous times by the pain. Choosing joy in the midst of it all sometimes takes mammoth effort—and faith in a reason to go on. But fortunately, we only have to choose it one day at a time—in fact, when it gets tough, only three minutes at a time. Choosing this joy, according to God's promise in Nehemiah 8:10 releases in us his strength to continue. Life and joy are a continuing choice. I share this mainly to let you know that I'm not an "expert" on peak performance. I struggle daily to be my best—and am frequently discouraged by the many areas in my life that still need improvement. My physical condition, for example, has deteriorated greatly since my accident—and I'm now struggling to get back into the shape I want to be in.

Perseverance is not an easy quality, yet it's not a quality for a select few. Most of the time, it involves an amount of courage that we would never believe we could have. It's a unique combination of patience plus endurance. It's what makes life worthwhile in spite of adversity. And quite often, it involves a quality of letting go and letting God keep us at it, funneling his power through us to keep us from quitting. I must confess that there are days I want to crawl into the corner and never come out.

However, I know full well that I don't have a corner on the pain market. I simply share these things to help us realize more fully that we all face tough times, emotionally and physically, and as we feel discouraged, we all think about giving up. At one time or another, giving up is exactly what we're all tempted to do in any undertaking or any crisis that stretches us, because such tough situations open us up to risk and failure.

Someone once told me a story about the devil giving a garage sale. He was selling quite a few tools he had used over the centuries. Some were barely used, others a little worn. But one was almost totally worn out. Some bargain-hunting soul picked up the worn-out tool and asked, "What is this?"

The devil replied, "Ooooh, that's been my favorite tool from the beginning. When nothing else works, I always use that." And he laughed devilishly.

The bargain hunter looked closer and saw, scratched on the tool's side, the word "Discouragement." Discouragement is something all of us wrestle with, and it is the sworn enemy of perseverance. But perseverance is the gift we're given to remind us we do have options. We can turn failures into personal successes; we can choose another option when all seems impossible; we can work miracles an inch at a time, by choosing to keep on moving, hoping, living. "Life," someone said, "is hard by the yard, but it's a cinch by the inch."

Sometimes perseverance is expressed in our waiting on God. I call this "wait training." As the Scriptures say, "they who wait for the Lord shall renew their strength, they shall mount up with wings like eagles, they shall run and not be weary, they shall walk and not faint" (Isaiah 40:31). Perhaps one of the greatest of sins is not waiting long enough, giving up too soon.

You may have heard the true story about the ten-year-old boy of a generation or two ago who, along with a friend, accidentally poured gasoline instead of kerosene on a stove fire in his little country schoolhouse. The stove blew up killing the other little boy instantly. The ten-year-old was so seriously injured the doctors wanted to amputate his legs.

But the boy's parents begged, "Give us just one more day." Each day, they asked for another day. And each day, the doctors hesitatingly gave it.

After months of living and hoping one day at a time, the doctors took off the bandages only to find that the boy's left leg was two and half inches shorter than his right leg, and his right foot was missing most of its toes. The doctors said, "This boy will never walk." But with perseverance, he walked. "He'll never walk without crutches," they said. But with perseverance, he walked without crutches. And then he broke into a wobbly jog. And then he decided to try running. And in a handful of years, this boy, Glen Cunningham, had become one of the greatest runners in Olympic history. In fact, he was once called "the world's fastest human being."

George Bernard Shaw had his first five novels rejected. Monet was painting great pictures at the age of 86. Tennyson wrote "Crossing the Bar" when he was 83. Composer Richard Wagner considered the first thirty years of his life a failure. His first, second, and third operas were dismal failures. These people not only persisted, they prevailed.

"But these are gifted people," you may say. Being gifted has very little to do with it. Maybe you and I haven't been given those bursts of genius, those flashes of inspiration, the blessing of exceptional talent. Yet I believe that our journey toward spiritual maturity, our creativity along the way, consists of small, deliberate, sometimes unnoticed steps. Amy Carmichael once penned these thoughts:

Sometimes when we read the words of those
who have been more
than conquerors, we feel almost despondent.

I feel that I shall never be like that.

But they won through step by step
by little bits of wills
little denials of self
little inward victories
by faithfulness in very little things.

They became what they are. No one sees these little hidden steps. They only see the accomplishment, but even so, those small steps were taken.

There is no sudden triumph
no spiritual maturity.
That is the work of the moment.

A little perseverance can add up to a lot of excellence. Glen Cunningham would have loved the shortest speech Winston Churchill ever gave. Churchill was asked back to his old school. Churchill, in fact, had been quite a failure at that very school; yet he found within himself a passion for excellence, a talent for turning failure into success through perseverance. And as you know, he became the prime minister of England and a heroic World War II figure.

As the schoolmaster introduced this man, one of the greatest orators of all time, to the auditorium full of schoolboys, he said, "Young men, be sure you take copious notes, because this will probably be one of the greatest speeches you'll ever hear." Do you know what the sum total of that message was that day? Short, stout Winston Churchill stood behind that podium and said, "Never give up!" And then he paused for almost a minute. Catching his breath, he continued even more boldly: "NEVER give up!" Another lengthy pause followed, and then, pounding his fist on the podium, he shouted at the top of his lungs: "Never, NEver, NEVer, NEVEr, NEVER GIVE UP!!!" And then he turned and quietly sat down. That was the sum total of his speech that day—perhaps one of the most unforgettable speeches of all time.

Chuck Swindoll calls it taking three steps forward and two steps back. To hope is to never give up. To see in even your most dismal failure a way to learn and grow is to never give up. To realize that a lifestyle based on peak performance—personally, spiritually, emotionally, mentally—is based on tapping into that special "power reserve" God has placed within us to know *why* we should never give up. Life is not meant to be painless, but it's not meant to be joyless, either. Persevere. Hang in there. It's the stuff of heroes, the hero within you.

14
Joy — the Master Skill

Joy is peace dancing.

These things I have spoken to you, that my joy may be in you, and that your joy may be full.　　　　　　　—*Jesus*

Joy is the flag flown high from the castle of my heart
　for the King is in residence there.　　—source unknown

Happiness turns up more or less where you'd expect it to—a good marriage, a rewarding job, a pleasant vacation. Joy, on the other hand, is as notoriously unpredictable as the One who bequeathed it.　　　　　　　—*Frederick Buechner*

The *key* principle, the one that gives life to all the others, is the ability to choose joy. If you don't have joy, you'll find it hard work to get anywhere in the first place. And if you do get there, without joy you won't be able to stay.

If you have that ability to enjoy your life, to enjoy your work, to feel an inner joy over the very fact of living, a power will flow throughout your plans and dreams, and you'll be living the peak performance process. The strength and the "want to" will be in place, and the rest will be much easier.

There is a direct relationship between joy and strength. When the Enemy wants to rob us of our strength, the first thing he will try to take away is our joy. Nehemiah 8:10 says that "the joy of the Lord is our strength." This implies that as you choose a millimeter of joy, God will give you an inch of strength, and that gives you the capacity to choose more joy. In return, the joy gives you the capacity to gain more strength. It is a process of continual choice, and continual empowering. As cycles go, this one is blessed indeed.

But what is joy? Is it the same as happiness? Not really. Joy is oftentimes a misunderstood concept. We get the picture of someone "jumping for joy"—"crying for joy"—"dancing for joy." But joy is something quite different.

1.   *Joy is not the same as happiness.*

Happiness depends on circumstances. In fact, the word itself comes from the same root word as *happening.* It means that something good has happened to you. For example, if I get a new shirt, I'm happy. If I eat a good meal, I'm happy. If I paid off my car, I'd be happy. In fact, I'd probably be *really* happy.

There's certainly nothing wrong with that. I encourage people to get as much happiness as they can—but we should realize that happiness is always based on circumstances, on "happenings."

Happiness is not the same as joy. Because circumstances allow happiness, they can also make happiness dissolve into thin air. Joy, on the other hand, defies circumstances. It can coexist with doubt, ambiguity, and pain. It is a contentedness beyond circumstances, an indestructible kind of confidence that says everything's all right even when everything looks, feels, and tastes all wrong. After one recent seminar, a woman came up to me and said, with profound insight: "*I never realized that I don't have to be happy to be joyful.*"

I may go so far as to say that you may not be able to have a lifestyle of joy without knowing pain in some intimate way. Author Lewis Smedes writes,

> You and I were created for joy, and if we miss it, we miss the reason for our existence. . . . If our joy is honest joy, however, it must somehow be congruous with human tragedy. This is the test of joy's integrity: is it compatible with pain? . . . *only the heart that hurts has a right to joy.*[15]

I asked a friend of mine what Scripture he thought of when he thought of joy. He said rather matter of factly, "The Sermon on the Mount."

Puzzled, I looked at him and said, "No, no. I said 'joy.'"

And he said, "Yeah, and I said, the Sermon on the Mount." He went on to explain that the word "blessed" actually implies the deepest quality of "joy" in the Greek. If we look again at the Sermon on the Mount and think of joy, we can begin to understand the deeper textures of joy—in poverty, persecution, and mourning, as well as in mercy and peacemaking. Joy has staying power. It's like an undercurrent, propelling us forward, no matter what's happening above.

In *You Gotta Keep Dancin'*, I wrote about joy in spite of circumstances. In it, though, I contend that before we can even consider such a notion we must first admit that pain is the universal reality of our human drama. I've never met anyone who doesn't know what pain is like. It's everywhere and in everything. As Sheldon Kopp once said, "Life can be counted on to provide all the pain that any of us might ever need."

Just as in the NASA terminology we mentioned earlier, it's "attitude" that determines where the pain will take us, and what it will produce within us. Will it be joy or will it be misery, will it be a prism or a prison? We can't avoid making a choice.

In 1962, Victor and Mildred Goertzel published a revealing study of 413 "famous and exceptionally gifted people" called *Cradles of Eminence.* They spent years attempting to understand what produced such greatness, what common thread might run through all of these outstanding people's lives. Surprisingly, the most outstanding fact was that virtually all of them, 392, had to overcome very difficult obstacles in order to become who they were.

Clyde Reid puts it this way:

> One of the most common obstacles to celebrating life fully is our avoidance of pain. We dread pain. We fear pain. We do anything to escape pain. Our culture reinforces our

avoidance of pain by assuring us that we can live a painless life . . . but to live without pain is to live half-alive . . . pain and joy run together. When we cut ourselves off from pain, we have unwittingly cut ourselves off from joy as well.[16]

Philippians, that short powerful epistle that was written after Paul had been shipwrecked and imprisoned, uses the word "joy" or "rejoice" over nineteen times. So surely we should understand that we don't have to wait until circumstances change to know joy.

As with good and bad, how would we know what joy felt like without knowing pain? There must have been a good reason for James to put joy and trials in the same sentence, for him to write something so outlandish as, "Count it all joy . . . when you meet various trials."

We tend to worry and scurry, attempting to avoid unhappiness, straining to be joyful, as if it was something we could *do*, instead of something we can *be*. We mutter things such as, "How can I be joyful when I know what happened last month?" or "I'll be joyful when all my problems work out, or when I feel better." We miss many of the chances to experience joy as an undercurrent of our days because of our desperate attempt to avoid pain, whether it be the emotional kind or the physical. People have asked me, "Which is worse—physical pain or emotional pain." I usually reply, "I think they're both lousy!" However, I suspect that in the long run emotional pain is more destructive and harder to deal with.

We don't get a free detour around problems when we become a Christian; we get a guided tour through them. 1 Thessalonians 5:18 says we're called to "rejoice always" and "give thanks *in* all circumstances; for this is the will of God in Christ Jesus for you" (italics mine). When we spend time regretting the past, and worrying about what the future will bring, we rush past God who is the ultimate source of joy. This beautiful poem says it all:

I AM

I was regretting the past
And fearing the future . . .
Suddenly my Lord was speaking:
"MY NAME IS I AM." He paused.
I waited. He continued,

"WHEN YOU LIVE IN THE PAST,
 WITH ITS MISTAKES AND REGRETS,
 IT IS HARD. I AM NOT THERE.
  MY NAME IS NOT *I WAS*.

"WHEN YOU LIVE IN THE FUTURE,
 WITH ITS PROBLEMS AND FEARS,
 IT IS HARD. I AM NOT THERE.
  MY NAME IS NOT *I WILL BE*.

"WHEN YOU LIVE IN THIS MOMENT,
 IT IS *NOT* HARD.
 I AM HERE.
  MY NAME IS *I AM*."
     —Helen Mallicoat

Joy is always in the present tense, just as God is, the Eternal *Now*. Psalm 16:11 reminds us that "in thy presence there is fullness of joy. . . ." Joy becomes real to us as a separate, constant entity apart from circumstances swirling around us only when we grasp the difference between it and come-and-go happiness. Joy is an opportunity and a gift now, if we choose it, and is meant to be as unchanging as the God from whom it flows.

 2. *Joy is a choice.*

Every single day since my accident, I am forced to consider how I might choose joy as a daily attitude. It's a constant choice. Some days the pain is so overwhelming that joyous is not what I want to be. Sometimes it's a demonic battle for me to choose joy for the next minute, much less the next day. And as I've said, choosing joy doesn't alleviate the pain, the ambiguity, and the doubt. It just gives us a way to live with it.

So now, on the days when the pain is scorching and there's not an ounce of joy to be had, I understand a very important principle—I know I'm miserable because I've chosen to be miserable. Therefore, I remind myself I do have another choice available to me. I *can* choose otherwise.

Sometimes those scorcher days almost paralyze me. I don't know what God is going to do with my body. What makes it harder, is that I come from a very athletic background. I once believed I could do just about anything physically I set my mind to. Now there are days I can't touch my knees or stand up straight without pain that makes my eyes water. Sometimes I can't keep the subtle and sometimes stifling fear down.

And yet, that fear is another reason I choose joy. Joy is like love. Joy knows no fear. Pastor Paul Sailhamer said "joy is that deep settled confidence that God is in control of every area of your life."

One time when I was asked to be on his radio program, Dr. James Dobson asked me why, after all this, do I choose joy? I said, "Because I've *got* to!" Sometimes I think I'd literally go to pieces if I didn't. I know that if I didn't choose joy my life would atrophy. The confidence that God is in control keeps me choosing it.

Joy, I've discovered, is a process in itself. It's more than a feeling. It's an attitude and a gift from our loving God. At first it's a conscious choice to live the next minute joyfully, then it's a prayer for more strength to choose joy, and then it's a mixture of the two. The joy and the prayer and the strength become somewhat of a habit, soon becoming a lifestyle. In its initial stages you choose to control your habits, but later those habits begin to control you. From the effort finally comes a sometimes quiet, sometimes exciting, confidence in the midst of the mess. That is joy.

Remember the 82-year-old pastor who had skin cancer so bad that he hid his face? Then one day, he read in Scripture where joy is a gift that Christ truly wants to give us (John 15:11)—and he made the choice to ask for it. And he got it. He got it in big gobs that shocked him so that he had to tell others. The joy was in the midst of the mess, and in spite of the mess—a choice and then a gift.

Life is tough; it's notoriously, atrociously difficult. So, accepting that fact, can you think of a better way to take on whatever life throws at you than joy? Nothing will affect your ability to live out life to the fullest as much as your inner commitment to joy.

Joy is free, but not cheap. It takes an intimate relationship with courage, with faith, and more often than not with pain. I once heard someone say, "Pain is inevitable, but misery is optional." I simply contend that joy is a better option, at the low points of your life as well as the high. And as you choose joy, it becomes easier to choose it the next minute, the next hour, the next day, the next year. When you've got joy, you've got it all.

3. *Joy is based on who we are and not what we have.*

If we were to believe the commercials and ads bombarding us daily—the Madison Avenue idea of joy—we'd believe that we had to be handsome or beautiful, smell great, style our hair a sexy way, drink a certain beverage, wear a certain designer's name on our clothes, visit exotic locations, and lead an all around glamorous life before our lives could be filled with joy. The thought of trying to keep up with all that makes me tired, not to mention a tad discouraged. The pull of the world is great, even when we know better.

We must be joyful now. Here . . . within . . . with who we are and what we've got.

Mark Speckman, a student athlete of mine during my Azusa Pacific University coaching days, knows the truth of that statement. I vividly remember the first day he came out for football. Mark was born with no hands. We all wondered how a guy with no hands could play football. He ended up not only being our starting middle linebacker, but in his senior year he was voted all-American. He used to love it when he would get called for holding. He would milk it for all it was worth with the refs. He also played the jazz trombone, basketball, and was a 3.6 student. We now play tennis together and we look forward to playing in a doubles tournament. I sometimes tell him jokingly that we will win half our games by our opponents' staring at him with wonder. Currently he's an outstanding coach and, when we can get him, he works as a Summit instructor. What made the difference? He decided to make life a challenge, and to tackle it all with joy. His joy is the source of his strength.

4. *Joy is not selfish.*

There's another reason to choose joy. When I'm miserable, I'm benefiting no one. Hence, I choose joy, oftentimes, for others' sake. Joy sets me free to turn outward.

Sometimes it takes everything you've got to even turn your face toward joy. But when there is a deeper purpose for joy, it can make all the difference during such tough times.

You see, when I don't choose joy, my choice is a selfish one. It's the same problem that occurs when I choose to wallow in my own guilt. One of the most powerful lines I've read recently is: "No one benefits from your guilt." I rob the world of my energy when I choose guilt. Likewise when I fail to accept myself, I rob the world of my ability to love. When I allow my misery to take over, when I become caught up in myself, I lock up God's energy within me. I imprison it within myself.

Self-pity is an awesome thing. Oftentimes, deciding to choose joy for myself is not enough to fend it off. Self-pity can keep coming back, whispering "Why me?" Trying to be joyful only for myself at such times is self-defeating. It won't work because it just won't last. Self-pity will not allow us to keep any joy that isn't tied to something bigger. Choosing joy for others, though, can give us a better, stronger reason not to give in.

Whether we like it or not, though, all of us have a built-in propensity to selfishness. That's what makes life so difficult. What other trait would have us cry, "Why me?" Left to our own devices, we will choose virtually everytime to do things for ourselves. If I choose joy for myself only, it has no staying power. It must be grounded in more than sheer selfishness. This is where grace comes in.

To truly understand joy, to choose it, and to have a realistic purpose for doing so, we need help—the help of grace. Philippians 2:13 tells how it works. "For it is God who is at work within you, giving you the *will* [my emphasis] and the power to achieve his purpose."

Think about this. The Christian life is not difficult. It's downright impossible. It's designed that way. If we could do it through achievements, we wouldn't need the grace of God.

Instead, we can say, "Thank you, Lord, for helping me choose joy for the sake of my wife, for the sake of my kids, for the sake of my friends." It's not something I could do for myself. Choosing joy and accepting the grace to keep it working sets me free to love. The purpose of joy is love and service, and we miss so much when we don't give our lives away in love.

Do you want to hear something that makes no sense at all, another paradox that's hard to explain? I've come to the point where in my own struggle I realize that my life is actually "ideal." I've been given this incredible "privilege" of pain because it has forced me to either give up or discover what real joy is all about. Otherwise, it's very possible that I never would have known true joy.

This realization comes in spurts, there's no doubt about that. But when I get my frame of reference correct and my priorities right, I understand exactly what James was talking about when he said to "consider it all joy," because I realize that such struggles pave the way to the gift of joy. They force us through the superficial crust of life to deeper inner peace. They are tools, you see, for discovering the deepest values there are in life and the deepest kind of joy that God gives.

5. *The purpose of joy is service.*

There is no way I could have ever understood this unless I had begun to understand that the ultimate purpose of joy is not to make us feel good. The purpose, you see, is to empower us, to give us stamina *to serve.* Personal peak performance becomes natural, becomes full and rich, when we understand this ultimate reason. Such joy, such peak performance, is to empower us to be *servant leaders*, as we'll be discussing in the next section.

Don't think for a moment that choosing joy for others is just another burden, another thing you "oughta" want to do as a Christian. That's a dead effort before it starts. Nobody in compassionate service is gritting his teeth. The term *reflex* could have been invented for the way that joy spreads around love and compassion, and how love and compassion spreads around joy.

A friend of mine once met Mother Teresa, the amazing woman who ministers to the dying on the putrid streets of Calcutta. My friend said she'd never met anybody so joyful. People ask Mother Teresa, "How do you do this awful work?" She always responds, "Awful work? What do you mean? I'm immensely privileged. I'm serving my Lord—tangibly." Matthew 25 says that when we serve the least of these, we serve Christ himself. Mother Teresa has made that verse her lifestyle. And her joy is legendary.

Do you believe joy is possible? A joyless Christianity is possible, I suppose, but it doesn't sound like too much fun. A joyless attempt at peak performance doesn't sound like too much fun either.

Did You Ever Doodle, Lord?

Lord,
did you ever do something silly,
just for the fun of it?

For example,
did you ever sit
and doodle in the air
floating somewhere
before you had this heavy world
upon your hands?

HOLY SWEAT

Did you ever let yourself go
and take a wild ride
across the galaxies
or tie a rainbow up in knots
without a thought
of just what someone else
might think of you?

Are the platypus and the kangaroo
a couple of favorite jokes
you kept around for laughs? . . .

Come on, God!
Let's set firecrackers
under every preacher and banker in town. . . .
Let's loosen up the world a bit
and use the fireman's hose
to knock the hats
off all those cats
who stiffen up their backs
and think they own this town.

Let's stop the traffic for a day
and have a ticker-tape parade
for all the orphans we have made.
Let's turn the land into a fair
and throw confetti in the air
to celebrate that you have come
to join us here.

Come on, God, let's go.

If Jesus Christ means anything
it means he's one of us.
And if his resurrection
isn't just a dream for dying men
then he's the one

who has to come
and bring this globe to life again.
—Norman C. Habel

All the concepts in this book are here-and-now stuff. Ordinary, commonplace blessedness. These ideas are things that can happen in your kitchen, in your backyard, in your office, in your plans and dreams. Joy is there. Joy is possible, as is the giddy gift of grace from which it springs.

The master gift of the Christian lifestyle—that's what joy essentially is. From it comes the urge to have a vision, to have courage and perseverance, to feel a passion for excellence, the willingness to risk and fail, and then the reason to give it all away.

I received a telegram one day. It said simply: UNTIL FURTHER NOTICE—CELEBRATE EVERYTHING!

15
Giving It All Away

This principle of our peak performance process is what sets this idea drastically apart from others. Our whole peak performance process is pointed toward this *ultimate* goal: We are called to become the very best version of ourselves we can possibly be, and then to give it all away to a world that is desperately hurting. We are called to share our lives with others.

Does this sound unusual? It shouldn't. It's the basis for our very faith. The peak performance *keys* as we have called them are to *release* us to be what the world desperately needs: servant leaders.

T. S. Eliot had a remarkable gift for words. He once said, "What we call the beginning is often the end. And to make an end is to make a beginning. The end is where we start from." Servant leadership is the beginning and the end of the peak performance process. It is the source and the ultimate goal.

What is a "servant leader"? A servant leader is a person who has a servant's heart and mind, a servant's values, a servant's attitude—and yet couples them all with the heart, skills, ingenuity, and problem-solving abilities of a leader. A servant leader is essentially someone willing to stand in the gap, someone who is willing to make a difference. Perhaps the saddest line in Scripture is this statement, spoken to Ezekiel by the Lord: "And I sought for a man among them, that should make up the hedge, and stand in the gap . . . *but I found none*" (Ezekiel 22:30 KJV italics mine).

Now is the time to roll up our sleeves and put what we believe is true into action. And that means *becoming* what we believe—embodying the values and fundamentals of our faith, making our theology into biography by reaching out to others. We've got to go from John 3:16, "For God so loved the world that he gave his only Son, . . ." to 1 John 3:17, "If I see a brother in need and do not do something about it, how can the love of God exist in me?" (my paraphrase). God's immense love must be translated to the world through us.

Someone once quipped: "For God so loved the world that he didn't send . . . a committee." In truth he loved us enough that he *gave* of his very essence, his very self. And we must take that to heart and let it seep out through our hands toward others. Jesus praised the widow who gave her last mite, not because of how much she gave, but because she held nothing back. We need to ask ourselves, what are we holding back? What are we still clinging to?

The world we live in is a hurting world, and we are called to do something about it. Two thousand years ago, God declared unambiguously in the life of Christ that human flesh is a good conductor of divine electricity and as far as I know he hasn't changed his mind. God still wants to use you and me to solve the world's problems—however outlandish that may sound. We've got to make our message true by the lives that we live.

This is the true joy in life, being used for a purpose recognized by yourself as a mighty one; being a force of nature instead of a feverish selfish little clod of ailments and grievances complaining that the world will not devote itself to making you happy.

I want to be thoroughly used up when I die, for the harder I work the more I live. I rejoice in life for its own sake. Life is no "brief candle" to me. It is a sort of splendid torch which I have got hold of for the moment, and I want to make it burn as brightly as possible before handing it on to future generations.[17]

In Ernest Gordon's true account of life in a World War II Japanese prison camp, *Through the Valley of the Kwai*, there is a story that never fails to move me. It is about a man who through giving it all away literally transformed a whole camp of soldiers. The man's name was Angus McGillivray.

Angus was a Scottish prisoner in one of the camps filled with Americans, Australians, and Britons who had helped build the infamous Bridge over the River Kwai. The camp had become an ugly situation. A dog-eat-dog mentality had set in. Allies would literally steal from each other and cheat each other; men would sleep on their packs and yet have them stolen from under their heads. Survival was everything. The law of the jungle prevailed. . . . until the news of Angus McGillivray's death spread throughout the camp. Rumors spread in the wake of his death. No one could believe big Angus had succumbed. He was strong, one of those whom they had expected to be the last to die. Actually, it wasn't the fact of his death that shocked the men, but the reason he died. Finally they pieced together the true story.

The Argylls (Scottish soldiers) took their buddy system very seriously. Their buddy was called their "mucker," and these Argylls believed that it was literally up to each of them to make sure their "mucker" survived. Angus's mucker, though, was dying, and everyone had given up on him, everyone, of course, but Angus. He had made up his mind that his friend would not die. Someone had stolen his mucker's blanket. So Angus gave him his own, telling his mucker that he had "just come across an extra one." Likewise, every mealtime, Angus would get his rations and take them to his friend, stand over him and force him to eat them, again stating that he was able to get "extra food." Angus was going to do anything and everything to see that his buddy got what he needed to recover.

But as Angus's mucker began to recover, Angus collapsed, slumped over, and died. The doctors discovered that he had died of starvation complicated by exhaustion. He had been giving of his own food and shelter. He had given everything he had—even his very life. The ramifications of his acts of love and unselfishness had a startling impact on the compound. "Greater love has no man than this, that a man lay down his life for his friends" (John 15:12).

As word circulated of the reason for Angus McGillivray's death, the feel of the camp began to change. Suddenly, men began to focus on their mates, their friends, the humanity of living beyond survival, of giving oneself away. They began to pool their talents—one was a violin maker, another an orchestra leader, another a cabinet maker, another a professor. Soon the camp had an orchestra full of homemade instruments and a church called the "Church Without Walls" that was so powerful, so compelling, that even the Japanese guards attended. The men began a university, a hospital, and a library system. The place was transformed; an all but smothered love revived, all because one man named Angus gave all he had for his friend. For many of those men this turnaround meant survival. What happened is an awesome illustration of the potential unleashed when one person actually gives it all away.

Try as we might, though, "giving it all away" can't be a thing we do out of duty. Otherwise, giving it all away is utterly impossible. You and I might give a little now and then. We might do our part to help others here and there. But giving it all, giving our all as a lifestyle, is thoroughly impossible on our own power. We can give all we can—but we can't give *all*.

The secret to this last principle is that it comes through

commitment more than through effort. As Dag Hammarskjöld reminds us in a profoundly simple way: "Not I, but God in me." It comes as an afterthought. Here is the most important part of our peak performance lifestyle, yet, it must be a result of the lifestyle itself. Joy is the key. Think of Angus McGillivray who gave himself away. The power, the reason he could do what he did was because of the joy he felt in saving his friend. *Joy is the platform* for giving it all away. How can you give it all if you don't have joy? Like grace, joy is a "given." Joy is the space in between the words and deeds. It is something that will happen as we grow in this peak performance lifestyle because it will come to seem the only logical, natural thing to do.

Still, "giving it all away" may sound like sacrifice. And sacrifice sounds so ultimate, so hard. You'll be surprised to know that the word comes from the root word *sacer-facere* which means "to make holy," to make whole. To take an idea and make it whole and holy is to put arms and legs and feet on it. Make it fulfilling. Make it real. And that's been our goal all along: wholiness.

I believe the world gets to know what Jesus looks like by looking at us, God's people. So I say, let's give them a good look. Let's live a life so powerful, so unsettling, so wonderful, so joyous, so giving, that our lives wouldn't make a bit of sense if God didn't exist.

We're called to be "people of the gap."

16
Your Own Peak Performance Points

Thus again, the Way will teach you the Way, and the Way is learning not to withhold yourself.   —*Bernard Phillips*

Each of our journeys is, as we've said, uniquely individual. The Christian experience is not a paint-by-the-numbers experience, no matter what we may be taught on occasion. To encourage you to add your own "steps" or "nudges" to the ten keys, jot down those personal ideas that work for you, in addition to the ten keys, in the blank space that follows here and on the next page.

Plus One — the Eleventh Key

Plus One
Solitude and Stillness—the Eleventh Key

We're always in process. True life is never static.

In the midst of writing this book and making the film series, I've been forced to grow and change in ways I hadn't expected. And I've discovered the obvious—many other keys could have been included in our list. That's one reason I've included this space for you to add your own keys.

But during this writing experience I've discovered one more key that I feel is absolutely critical to this lifestyle. I'd like you to consider it.

The challenge we hear so often today (it's even implied within these pages) is: "Do more! Give more! Be more! Go for it!"

I think we need that challenge to move us out of our cul-de-sacs of mediocrity, to encourage us to find and fulfill our calling. But in the midst of all this excitement, God also speaks (another paradox, perhaps) to us very clearly: "Be *still*, and know that I am God" (Psalm 46:10).

The ultimate call is not that we are committed to a task, but to a Person. There's a time to roll up your sleeves, but that time must also be matched with a time to be still, to listen—which is the core of obedience. In fact, the word *obedience* comes from the root *oboedire*, which means "to listen."

I enjoy myself most when I am so at peace that activity is secondary . . . necessitating a heart which consistently yields itself to its source. Centering is the image I use for

151

the process of balance which enables us to step along that thread feeling it not as a thread but a sphere. It will, it is hoped, help us to walk through the necessary extremes with an incorruptible instinct for wholeness. . . . This thread can be as limber as breath. It can be as tough as a wild grapevine.

—M. C. *Richards*

There is a time to start, and there is a time to stop, wait, be stilled, and be centered in our Lord. "There's nothing quite so nauseating or pathetic as the flesh trying to be holy," exclaims Major Ian Thomas.

In the world we learn compassion, but in silence we learn the music that directs our acts. In silence more than anywhere else we are given access to our possibilities.

In a world that victimizes us by its compulsions, we are called to solitude where we can struggle . . . and let our new self be born in the loving encounter with Jesus Christ. It is in this solitude that we become compassionate people, deeply aware of the solidarity of our brokenness with all humanity and ready to reach out to anyone in need.[18]

As we continue our journey, we eventually come to the place where stillness and action intersect and become one—for the true contemplative is a person of action. Likewise, those committed to utilizing all their possibilities to serve Christ in the world must come from the place of stillness.

> I need time
>   uncluttered time
>   to center myself
>   to gather myself in—
>
> I want to find the center again,
>   that will keep my life together.

I want to look into my own eyes
   to become quiet
      in order to be able to love again.

God offers Himself as center
   as axis around which all revolves
      as the core of all things.

He *is* the circle
   in which we are all *free* —
   And in the circle,
      the cross
   onto which we fall
And from which we rise again
   to a life of love.

                —Ulrich Schaffer

PART THREE

PEOPLE OF THE GAP
BEING A JOYFUL, COMPETENT,
COMPASSIONATE SERVANT LEADER

The "How" of Holy Sweat

I sought for a man to stand in the gap and there was none.
                                              —Ezekiel 22:30

I want to know God's thoughts.   —*Albert Einstein*

A good and generous man wanted to teach his son and his daughter about servant leadership, so he entrusted the two with a special mission of mercy. Their task was to distribute food to the peasants of a nearby village who were suffering from starvation due to severe famine. Both were given the same instructions, the same amount of supplies, and the same quota of people to feed.

The son approached his task with deep commitment and resolve. Besides helping the people, he wanted to complete the task quickly and efficiently so that he might please his father. He was determined to be objective about his task, so he organized his assignment with great skill. His organization and objectivity paid off, and he was able to return to his father's house by midday with his assignment completed.

The daughter was not nearly as efficient or objective. As she began distributing the food, she became deeply moved by the starving people. Soon, she found herself immersed in the people's needs. As a result she took hours longer than her brother to distribute her food, and she returned to her father's house weary, her eyes red and swollen from weeping, her body weak from her own hunger. She was shivering all over because she had given her coat and her shoes away to others.

When the two were called before their father to report of their mission, the son confidently reported that his mission of distribution had been completed efficiently and that everyone had received food in a short time. The daughter gave her report haltingly and with deep emotion, talking at length about the many other needs the peasants had beyond food.

Which of these was the true servant leader?

The answer? It's difficult to say. Perhaps both. The true servant leader is a blessed blend of the two—the compassion of one and the effectiveness of the other. The servant leader should not only be highly committed, and highly compassionate, but also highly trained. Yet we don't seem to have a good grasp of what that training should be. On one hand, we sometimes offer leadership training that is actually secular in its principles, with a Christian veneer—the type that would applaud the efficiency-minded son and support what he did with citations from Scripture. Or we teach that Christians should be most like the compassionate, servant-minded daughter, praising her emotion while overlooking the very needed leadership qualities of the son. Yet, what our world is crying for is a dynamic, effective blend of the two.

Servant leaders are this blend of compassion and effectiveness. They are people of the gap, called to stand in the gap and bridge it wherever and whenever they can, however they can. That's the kind of leadership that our continuing peak performance lifestyle must result in.

So far, I've offered some initial ways to discover and make the lifestyle your own. Now, I want to express *how* I believe it can be lived out—the life God intended us to live as we discover our best through him.

This both/and paradox of the nature of servant leadership is brilliantly captured in the following words by Philip C. Brewer:

Paradoxes of a Man of God

Strong enough to be weak;
Successful enough to fail;
Busy enough to take time;
Wise enough to say, "I don't know";
Serious enough to laugh;
Rich enough to be poor;
Right enough to say, "I'm wrong";
Compassionate enough to discipline;
Conservative enough to give freely;
Mature enough to be childlike;
Righteous enough to be a sinner;
Important enough to be last;
Courageous enough to fear God;
Planned enough to be spontaneous;
Controlled enough to be flexible;
Free enough to endure captivity;
Knowledgeable enough to ask questions;
Loving enough to be angry;
Great enough to be anonymous;
Responsible enough to play;
Assured enough to be rejected;
Stable enough to cry;
Victorious enough to lose;
Industrious enough to relax;
Leading enough to serve.

—Philip C. Brewer

17
What Is a Servant Leader?

He who is greatest among you shall be your servant. . . .
—Matthew 23:11

Of this I am certain. The only ones among you who will be truly happy are those who have sought and found how to *serve.*
—*Albert Schweitzer*

"Servant leader." It's another paradox, isn't it? How can you be a servant and a leader? Doesn't one cancel out the other? The two may seem totally incompatible at first glance.

Let's explore the two words. The idea of being a "servant" doesn't sound too attractive to our North American ears, does it? But the idea of being a "leader"—well, that's right up our alley. Being a leader sounds good to us freedom-lovers.

Being a servant, though, sounds too much like being a slave for most of us. During a seminar, a Christian doctor winced when I began talking about servant leadership. "Can't we call it something else?" he said.

But here's another paradox. Servant leaders are the freest of all leaders. E. Stanley Jones believes that "self-surrender is the greatest emancipation that ever comes to a human being. Seek first the kingdom of God," he says, "and all things will be added to you—including yourself." *If you don't seek the kingdom first, you don't seek it at all.* Servant leaders know why they lead and how to lead. And they know Who they lead for. They lead because they've already learned Who they are emulating: the Christ who taught that the greatest shall be the least, the first shall be last, and then took out a towel and began washing his disciples' feet. There never lived a freer man. That is where the servant leader's freedom comes from.

Earlier I mentioned that "a servant leader is one who has a servant's heart and mind, a servant's values and attitudes, but a leader's skill, a leader's vision and ingenuity, and a leader's creativity." A leader in its simplest definition has two primary ingredients. He is (1) influencing people (2) in a certain direction. That direction may be positive or negative. Obviously, a servant leader differs from the average, everyday leader in several ways, but the main difference is not so much outward as inward.

Robert Greenleaf, in his book *Servant Leadership*, which is concerned about a servant attitude in business, tells a story first found in Hermann Hesse's *Journey to the East*. In the story, a band of men are on a journey commissioned by one of those mysterious orders, an isolated group of cloistered men found now and again in the lands of the East. Leo, a servant accompanying the traveling party, does menial chores for them, and also sustains them with his spirit and his song. He is a man of extraordinary presence. While he is in camp, the group feels a peace and a solidarity they are quite unaware of—until Leo mysteriously disappears. Then the group falls into disarray, and the journey is finally abandoned. They now realize how important the mysterious Leo was to their success.

After some years of wandering, one of the men finds Leo and is taken into the Order. There he discovers that Leo, whom he has known first as a servant, is in fact the actual head of the Order, its guiding spirit, its great leader.

"Leo was actually the leader all the time," Greenleaf explains, "but he was servant first because that was what he was, *deep down inside.*" That was the key to his effectiveness and his greatness. Leo's grasp of servant leadership came effortlessly, because it came from within.

A servant leader, then, is a servant first. But he or she is a servant in the very best meaning of the word—someone who has chosen to give his or her talents and time to God and to others.

Jesus was the greatest leader of all time. Yet Jesus had a servant's heart and a servant's compassion.

Frederick Buechner once said, "Compassion is that sometimes fatal capacity for feeling what it's like to live inside somebody else's skin. It is the knowledge that there can never be any joy and peace for me until there is joy and peace for you as well." A servant leader will adopt a Bob Pierce sort of compassion. The founder of World Vision lived by the motto: "May my heart break with the things that break the heart of God."

The Bible says in Matthew 9 that when Jesus saw the people he had compassion for them. The Greek word for "compassion" in this Scripture means "to suffer with," which implies he cared so much it physically affected him. It's as if he almost retched, because he was so deeply concerned.

We need to care so much that we'll figure out ways to help. We need to see the world through Christ's eyes, and then do something about what we see, educating our compassion, putting feet and hands to it. That takes someone with the skills and heart of a servant leader.

But one look at the world through Christ's eyes will make most of us throw up our hands. Look how complex, how devastating the needs are! Many of us choose to bury our heads in the sand in response.

But if Scripture is true, and I obviously believe it is, then we have no option. We *must* become involved. We are to fill those gaps, if we do it only one pothole at a time. Tom Sine in his brilliant book *The Mustard Seed Conspiracy* says, "God has always chosen to change the world through the lowly, the unassuming and the imperceptible." It's always been God's strategy to use ordinary people like you and me.

The gaps are everywhere. Economic gaps, emotional gaps, sociological gaps, spiritual gaps. And I think many people are working hard right now to fill them. But to recognize the gaps, we've got to see them. Our world's troubles are so overwhelming, we toughen ourselves and close our eyes. It's not easy to find the gaps with our eyes closed.

I overheard a story that has had a powerful effect on my understanding of just how hardened Christian people can become in order to protect themselves from seeing the engulfing hurt and need. One semester, a seminary professor set up his preaching class in an unusual way. He scheduled his students to preach on the Parable of the Good Samaritan and on the day of class, he choreographed his experiment so that each student would go, one at a time, from one classroom to another where he or she would preach a sermon. The professor gave some students ten minutes to go from one room to the other; to others he allowed less time, forcing them to rush in order to meet the schedule. Each student, one at a time, had to walk down a certain corridor and pass by a bum, who was deliberately planted there, obviously in need of some sort of aid.

The results were surprising, and offered a powerful lesson to them. The percentage of those good men and women who stopped to help was extremely low, especially for those who were under the pressure of a shorter time period. The tighter the schedule, the fewer were those who stopped to help the indigent man. When the professor revealed his experiment, you can imagine the impact on that class of future spiritual leaders. Rushing to preach a sermon on the Good Samaritan they had walked past the beggar at the heart of the parable. We must have eyes to see as well as hands to help, or we may never help at all. I think this well-known poem expresses it powerfully:

> *I was hungry and you formed a humanities club*
> *to discuss my hunger.*
> Thank you.

> *I was imprisoned and you crept off quietly*
> *to your chapel to pray for my release.*
> Nice.

*I was naked and in your mind you debated the
morality of my appearance.*
What good did that do?

*I was sick and you knelt and thanked God for
your health.*
But I needed you.

*I was homeless and you preached to me of the
shelter of the love of God.*
I wish you'd taken me home.

I was lonely and you left me alone to pray for me.
Why didn't you stay?

*You seem so holy, so close to God; But I'm still
very hungry, lonely, cold, and still in pain.*
Does it matter?

—Anonymous

Here's where the development of a servant leader's qualities comes in. I firmly believe that a servant leader must develop such qualities in a deliberate order to be effective. Watch the drawings that follow.

First, we must train the eyes to see the world differently. We must cultivate *awareness*, the talent of seeing the world as Christ sees it.

I don't wear glasses, but some years ago, as an experiment in trying to learn how to see the world through Christ's eyes, I put on an old pair of wire-rim glasses, with no lenses. I would wear them for a couple of hours at a time with the prayer: "Lord, teach me how to see the world the way you see it." I've done this now for years as a holy reminder—to try to see the world through Christ's eyes. I mention this only as a suggestion; perhaps you'll invent your own way to do it. But this first step, *awareness*, is absolutely critical.

AWARENESS

Then, when we can see the need, we consequently feel motivated, and it touches our hearts. We are moved to do something about what we see, to care enough to be involved. A friend of mine who is involved in inner-city youth work insists, "If I could just get people to come down here and look my kids in the eyes, I have no question that they would get involved." *Motivation follows awareness.*

MOTIVATION

Often, we are good at this part. But the tough part is that much of our Christian leadership ends right here. Many times we'll motivate our young leaders right out of college and seminary to get out there and *see* and *feel* . . . but once they are out there and find that those are the only "tools" they've been given, they often cannot handle it. Sadly, they haven't been taught any of the other skills they desperately need, not just to be effective, but to survive.

I know one young man whom I taught in a seminary course who was red-hot with motivation for ministry. In fact, I'd never seen someone so on fire for Christ. His compassion compelled him to work with some of the deepest hurts of the inner city. The tragedy was that he was so unprepared for the complexities of the problems there that he burned out. He not only left the work, but eventually the faith. As I understand it, the latest figures show that a huge percentage of our young missionaries eventually drop out of mission work and go home. Perhaps it's because we're not teaching leadership skills to go with our servant heart.

That's where the next drawing comes in—the hands and feet appear. These represent the leadership skills, feet to lead and hands to solve problems. The core of life and, therefore, the core of Christian life is solving problems. In all my years of teaching on high school, university, and seminary levels, I've been shocked at how little is understood about the problem-solving process. When I've asked students to give me an actual step-by-step plan for solving problems, I have never received a logical, cogent plan. A servant leader needs these skills.

SKILL

Last of all, there's a smile. There's the joy, which supplies the power and the stamina. With the eyes, a servant leader sees the gap; with the heart, the servant leader decides to fill the gap; with the hands, the servant leader works to fill the gap; with the feet, the servant leader stands in the gap. In fact, watch those feet. Generally speaking, if you really want to know who you are, distinct from whom you like to think you are, *keep an eye on where your feet take you.*

POWER

As the final drawing shows, we must bind with others, as the loving body of Christ, to bridge the gap.

We may believe that we are fully formed as servant leaders without this last element. But it's not true. There are no Lone Ranger servant leaders.

"I am more than I am, *but less than we are.*" There's an "us-ness" to the Christian faith that we cannot deny. Community and teamwork: These give us the encouragement and the concrete direction to become involved as we are called to. We don't have to wait until we're "perfect" to get involved. Working with other servant leaders reminds us of that. We are all the broken body of Christ, and it's in our brokenness that we're called to be "wounded healers."

Servant leadership, of course, is still a process, just as the peak performance lifestyle it springs from. In the midst of our own brokenness, in the midst of our own poverty, in the midst of our own growing, we're still learning. The point of servant leadership is that we are constantly getting involved, constantly developing and deepening our compassion, our joy, and our competence.

In essence, the drawings show three essential elements of the servant leader: *compassion, joy,* and *competence.* We are to be compassionate, joyful, competent servant leaders: *compassion,* for the urge to be there, and the heart to reach out—*joy* for stamina, to be able to give freely and keep giving freely—*competence,* for staying power, to truly help in solving problems.

18
What Is Our Model for Being a Servant Leader?

When Jesus gathered His disciples for the Last Supper they were having trouble over which one was the greatest. Gathered at the Passover feast, the disciples were keenly aware that someone needed to wash the others' feet. The problem was that the only people who washed feet were the least. So there they sat, feet caked with dirt. It was such a sore point that they were not even going to talk about it. No one wanted to be considered the least. Then Jesus took a towel and a basin *and so redefined greatness.*
—*Richard Foster*

Kaki Logan, one of our finest instructors, tells a powerful but familiar story in a refreshing way:

"Suppose you were a VIP. Suppose, in fact, you were a very, very, *very* important person. The biggest of big shots. Not just locally known, or nationally known, but world renowned. You've been working on a special leadership project for a few years and have handpicked a few good people to continue your vision. You've dedicated the last several years of your life to teaching them these principles.

"Now suppose that it's your last night in town. You'll never see these people again. What would you do? How would you act with this select group on that last night? Would you hand out a notebook with a summary of all your principles in it, the most important ones marked with a yellow pen? Would you show a slide presentation to give them an effective visual aid for what you've been trying to teach them? Or would you give them an inspiring, heart-rending lecture? There are lots of options, all of which might be effective. At this point, most of us would be ready for some sensational event or some sensational utterance. But would you even dream of picking up a cloth, and instructing them to take off their shoes and socks so you could wash their feet?"

Jesus of Nazareth—this Jesus whom we so often fail to comprehend—what did he do on his last night in town? Exactly! He washed his disciples' dirty, grimy, musty feet. At that time, footwashing was one of the most humble acts one could do. It was an act meant not just for slaves, but for the lowest class of slaves. So, Jesus didn't *tell* his men about servant leadership; he *enacted* it.

Yet in the scene just before this, described in John 12, Jesus makes the statement that all power in heaven and earth is available to him. He says in essence, "If you want to see the Father, look at me." Here he is, claiming more power and more authority than any king, any ruler, any rabbi alive, and the very next thing we read of him doing is performing an act normally relegated to those lowest on the servant totem pole.

This is the amazing paradox that we must explore, not only with our minds, but with our lives. Jesus' washing those sweaty men's feet was not an act of servile weakness, but an unbelievably potent act of strength. It was a demonstration of the very character of God. God on his knees.

Jesus told us that if we want to know what God is like, we should look at him. And so we can see that God serves out of strength, out of boldness. Washing the disciples' feet was such an audacious act that Peter, who became one of the greatest leaders of all time, told Christ, "You'll never wash my feet, Lord." He was that stunned. However, Jesus said, "Then you'll never get into the kingdom." To that Peter replied, "Then, Master, wash me from head to toe!"

When Jesus finished washing the disciples' feet, what did he do? He motioned for them to do likewise. The Christ of the New Testament is the living embodiment of servant leadership, and his life is the model we need for the servant leadership he calls us to.

- "The first shall be last."
- "The greatest shall be the least."
- "The greatest of you shall be a servant."

These are only a few of his words we are called to live by. We've got to allow such Scriptures to be real and alive. We aren't just to believe this truth; we are to do it.

The first shall be last. That's always been a confusing statement for me. I've thought it sounded nice and had an interesting, poetic ring to it, but I never understood what it meant in its practical application. Then it dawned on me. If we are truly encouragers in the same servant sense as Christ was, we will be automatically pushing others ahead of ourselves. We are enabling them, encouraging them, empowering them. If I do that with Erma, Jim, Danielle, Peb, Rick, Lois, Jack, Pam, Zac, and Josh, then where will I end up? Last! Because I'm pushing others to be their best. The one who has mastered the servant leadership concept, is the last naturally. Such are the upside-down values of the kingdom of God.

An exercise I use at times in seminars seeks to persuade the participants to consider their values. I tell them, "You have exactly two minutes to line up in order of importance." Well, the group bursts into panic. "Importance according to what?!" they have to ask each other. I remember one guy who smugly thought he had me figured out and walked proudly to the humble spot at the back of the line. Another man grabbed a pregnant lady and put her in front, explaining that there's nothing more important than that, and then told everybody else to line up according to height. There are hundreds of ways to respond, but more than anything, the question forces the participants to consider what is really "important."

I believe that is what God is asking us daily. What really is important? The standard by which we must compare and contrast our values is the Bible's account of Christ's life.

Without Christ's life as a touchstone, our servant leadership could easily become just another tag, another achievement. And of course, that is the danger I spoke of in the Introduction. Once you think you've really "arrived" at servant leadership, you have missed the point. It's like being proud of your humility. We have a touchstone, and his life reminds us over and over that servant leadership is a continuing journey in which we continue to grow in freedom and truth.

John 8:32 says, "You shall know the truth and the truth shall make you . . . ." Happy? No. "You shall know the truth and the truth shall make you. . . ." Successful? Popular? Important? Intelligent? No. "You shall know the truth and the truth shall make you *free.*" When we mix the truth with freedom, we begin to understand how we can be free enough to be a servant leader—then we can give ourselves away in the name of Christ.

The psychologist Erich Fromm says that giving is perhaps the greatest act of potency in our lives. If I give to you, that means I have more than enough. I am overflowing. And this is where joy comes in. Giving is a reflex. It's not a task, an "okay, if I gotta" sort of dutiful act. It's done out of freedom and with an overwhelming desire.

Like joy, giving multiplies when it is divided with others. Such is the new math of the kingdom.

Back in my high school teaching days, some years after I became a Christian, I remember a situation that still reminds me of this unusual reflex action that goes along with following Christ. One day the principal stopped me and said, "Hansel, I can't figure you out. I've been watching you for the last eight months. You stay after school and hang around with all the messed-up and troubled kids. Why do you do that? Why do you spend so much of your own time with these dead-end kids?"

I said, "Well, I don't know. I can't help it, I guess."

"I don't understand," he said.

"Do you really want to know why I do it?" I asked.

"Yes," he said.

"Look, I don't know where you are in this area of your life, Sir, but ever since I've gotten involved with this Jesus, I can't help but hang around with people like that. It seems to be an impulse, a reflex. It just seems that these are the ones he wants me to hang around with." It was what I *wanted* to do, because of how I felt, and what I understood, about Jesus—not some obligation or duty. The urge certainly didn't come out of my own goodness. It was part of an overflowing from my relationship with Christ. And it was all aimed toward God. By that, I mean, we must remember that as we serve others, we are essentially, emphatically serving God first and foremost.

Above all, above everything—your primary responsibility is your relationship with Christ. Then next, as you become so connected to and empowered by God through Jesus Christ, you give naturally out of overflow. If you *try* to give, if you *try* to be a servant leader, you will never be able to keep it up. Human ambition alone can't sustain it. What we are talking about is arriving at a level in your relationship with Jesus Christ at which you want to be like him so much that you cannot help but give yourself away. You let go. He is your model and *the source* of the only power you need to live as a servant leader.

What Does a Servant Leader Do?

Are we talking about witnessing, then? Is that what a servant leader is supposed to do?

I was asked to speak at a pre-Billy Graham Crusade evangelistic conference. I was speaking to hundreds of people who were there for the express purpose of evangelism. My opening sentence to them was, "I'm going to do everything in my power tonight to try and get you *not* to do witnessing." The pastors on the front row went ashen grey. People's faces all over the crowd looked shocked. My staff thought I had finally gone off my rocker. But I had their attention.

Then I said, "What does Acts 1:8 say? It says, 'Be my

witnesses.' That's not just a semantic difference. That's a critical and essential difference. There is a distinct difference between *doing* and *being* a witness. Unless you are 'being' a witness, none of your 'doing' will matter."

Harvard did a study on nonverbal communication and came up with over seven hundred thousand different ways to communicate nonverbally. That means, of course, that if we're trying to communicate Christ with words only, we are up against odds of seven hundred thousand to one.

For example, if I walk up to you and say, "It's really nice to meet you," but all the while I'm looking at my watch or glancing behind you at someone else, what message are you going to believe? My words or my actions? "*Be* my witnesses." Basically, to *be* witnesses means to express Christ with our lives. And I believe the epitome of doing that is as a servant leader.

In his book *The Fight*, John White asks, "Is witnessing something you are or something you say or something you do?" He answers:

> A witness is something you are, but what you are always determines what you say or do. The three—being, saying, and doing—are part of a whole. Essentially, a witness is someone who is truthful about what he has seen, heard, and personally experienced. Moreover, the witness of Jesus must not only tell the truth, but live it.[19]

In essence, a servant leader is a *signpost*. That's how White goes on to describe the dedicated witness. And the image is wonderful for explaining the true nature of the servant leader's public role.

Think about it. What does a signpost do? You don't point to one and say, "Man, what a *hot* looking signpost! I wonder what its I.Q. is? Listen to how brilliantly the signpost speaks! Look at the figure on that signpost!" A signpost serves a singular purpose—it points you to the way you want to go. All that matters is that its lettering is bold and clear and that it's pointing in the right direction.

"A signpost has defeated its purpose if it is so attractive that it draws attention to itself," explains White. That is true. We are meant to be signposts for Christ in the sense that the critical purpose of our lives is not what people think of us, but that they think of Jesus Christ because of us. As signposts, we should be almost invisible, pointing the way to the visible Christ.

We are to make the invisible Christ more visible in all that we do. That is one of my lifetime goals. It is a daily struggle of letting go.

19
What Is the Power Source for Being a Servant Leader?

Just as each of us has a unique fingerprint, so each of us has a unique inner personal gift. We are all the poorer if we do not encourage it to be released in others, nor release our own.

Jesus is calling us into a new community where *leadership will be measured in terms of effective facilitation of others*; where our task will be not to share our riches with others, but to *reveal their riches to them.*
—*Robert Raines*

By now, you may be rolling your eyes, wondering if this whole, lofty idea of servant leadership is actually possible for you. Even though we've talked repeatedly about how the lifestyle becomes reflex as you discover the daily life of the peak performance process, you may still wonder about such an amazing transformation.

In the Introduction, I explained the concept of Holy Sweat and why I believe that term to be perfect for a book that invites the reader on an adventure to discover the servant leader within. By now I hope the image Holy Sweat conjures up is of "grace with blisters," of holiness that believes in getting its hands dirty, of a commitment with talent, courage, vision, and passion all rolled up in one potent package.

Holy Sweat is all of those. But most of all, Holy Sweat is a faith that has come to realize that *sanctification* is a process and not just an event.

What do I mean by that? You've heard the word a thousand times before. Sanctification. It is the key to the transformation that takes place within the person who makes that Holy Sweat commitment to be his or her best. I believe Frederick Buechner, in his jewel of a book, *Wishful Thinking*, explains the reality of that biblical term best. Salvation is a "two-step process," he explains, not a "one-time event." We are meant not only to be justified (step one) but to become Christlike (step two).

In the experience of St. Paul, only when persons discover that God really loves them, in all their unloveliness (justification), do they begin to take on the attributes of the One who justified them.

As Buechner points out, Paul's word for the gradual transformation of this sow's ear into a silk purse is "sanctification." Paul sees it as this second vital step. Buechner explains our transformation so well:

> Being sanctified is a long and painful stage because with part of himself the sinner prefers the sin. . . . Many drop out with the job hardly more than begun and among those who stay with it there are few if any who don't drag their feet most of the way.
>
> But little by little—less by taking pains than by taking it easy—*the forgiven man starts to become a forgiving man, the healed man to become a healing man, the loved man to become a loving man* [my italics]. God does most of it. The end of the process, Paul says, is eternal life.[20]

The forgiven man becomes a forgiving man! The healed man a healing man! The loved man a loving man! Isn't that an incredibly real image of us?

But I also see myself in his image of "foot dragging." And I know you do, too. No one is different. As Buechner points out, those who hang in there are, little by little, transformed. "God does most of it," he says. As we hang in there, keep to our commitment, the little-by-little transformation is what turns us into joyful, compassionate, and competent servant leaders. It's true. If I had not seen it happen time and time again I would not dare write about it.

Profile of a Servant Leader

I know it would be helpful to have an idea of the way a servant leader goes about giving himself away. We *can* list some tangible ways a servant leader leads his or her life that can give you a good idea of how to shape your own:

1. *A servant leader knows how to recognize and celebrate the differences in others and in him-/herself.*

The beauty of God's plan is that he made us all different. I am the only version of Tim Hansel that has ever been and will ever be. I know many people who are relieved to hear that news. But the same can be said of you, of everyone.

Have you ever thought about this? Nobody else will have the same relationship that you have with Jesus Christ. Yours is absolutely, positively unique. No wonder we all express it differently.

Just as our relationship with Christ is unique, so is the life he's given us. This life is our one unique shot. As I've said throughout the book, being the best version of me that I can be is the only way to live that one shot. So, that uniqueness transfers into my life as a servant leader. I'm simply called to be a servant leader by my own design. I'm not to imitate anyone. I'm to take such ideas as the ones listed here and incorporate them into my own unique situation and style.

2. *A servant leader has "nothing to prove, nothing to lose."*

There is so much pressure to conform, especially in evangelical Christian circles. But the book of Romans tells us to be committed nonconformists. "Don't let the world around you squeeze you into its own mold, but let God remold your minds from within, so that you may prove in practice that the plan of God for you is good, meets all his demands and moves toward the goal of true maturity" (Romans 12:2 PHILLIPS). Cookie-cutter Christianity is not for us. We need to be different. We have "nothing to prove and nothing to lose; we're called to be *unsqueezed* followers of Christ," as Chuck Swindoll has put it. A servant leader has nothing to prove to anyone and nothing to lose, so he or she is free to live a unique life to the fullest. Ours is not a duty, but an incredible privilege. I don't have to worry whether you like me or not. That's not the purpose of being a servant leader. I am following another Voice. I am playing to an "Audience of One." And I am told to celebrate the differences in myself and in others.

The moment I am free to celebrate my own differences, I can help others celebrate theirs, finding ways to enable them and myself in a positive way.

3. *A servant leader is an encourager.*

It is surprising what a difference attitude will make in working with others. A servant leader is tolerant and has a good eye for others' best qualities—and then celebrates them. Enables them. Enhances them. Encourages them. There are two types of people who enter a room—one who says, "Here I am," and one who says, "There *you* are." Which are you more attracted to? And which could encourage you more?

How often do we pass up opportunities to encourage others? I'm reminded of an event that changed this area of my life forever. During the Christmas holidays a few years ago, I decided to visit a very large church, with three or four thousand members, in order to hear a special performance of a Bach oratorio. I love baroque music. The performance was absolutely stunning. At the conclusion, I felt compelled to congratulate the elderly man who had conducted the entire performance and had played the organ for it as well. In my exuberance, I actually grabbed the man's arm and exclaimed, "It was wonderful! It made my whole Christmas season! It was the best performance I've ever heard!"

His response, though, caught me completely off guard. He began to cry. And I, being a supposed "survival expert," did the appropriate thing. *I absolutely panicked.* I stammered, apologizing profusely, feeling awful for upsetting the man. "I'm sorry," I kept saying, "Really . . . I'm sorry for whatever I said. Uh, what was it I said? I'm not from this church. I'm a visitor."

I tried my best to disappear into the crowd. But as I was

backing away, he grabbed my sleeve, still wiping his eyes. When he finally regained his composure, he said, "Son, you just caught me by surprise."

"Sir, I don't think I understand. What do you mean?" I said.

"Well . . . ," he spoke hesitatingly with tears in his eyes, "You see, I've been here eighteen years and you are the *first* person who's ever done that."

I was flabbergasted. That night I went home, got on my knees and asked God to help me never overlook another opportunity to encourage others. A servant leader is, if nothing else, an encourager, one who "puts courage into" another. That's what community is all about. We need to remind each other of the Christ who lives within us.

Sometimes it's easier for me to see Christ in others than it is to see Christ in myself. Like this morning. When I got up, I felt so bad that I walked into the bathroom, looked in the mirror, and said, "Oh, Lord, re-deal!" But when others see Christ in me, and tell me so, I cannot express how much it means to me. It reminds me Whose I am. Talk about encouragement! The following poem by Norman Habel says it better than I've ever heard it expressed:

Some Very Special People

I want to thank you, Lord, for some special people that I
    love,
Special people who love me just because I'm me,
People who believe that I'm important, as I am,
People who can stand me even when I'm sour and
    disgusting,
People who listen when I spit out my feelings,
People who wait when I cannot find the words,
People who shake me when my spirit falls asleep.

For all those very special people
I want to shout
And shout and shout with thanks.

Those are the people, one today, one tomorrow,
Who look for that part of me that's me,
Who groan with me until that part of me is free,
Who will love whatever is left of me when the day is
   over.

For all those very special people
I want to sing
and sing and sing with love.

For ones like that, Lord, mean more to me
than anything on earth, and sometimes even more than
   you.
For only through someone like that do I believe that you
   are really true.
[For] when someone like that accepts me in my sorry
   little mess,
Then so do you, my Lord,
Then so do you . . . .

4.   *A servant leader lives daily to reflect and re-present Christ
in the world.*

A little boy came home from Sunday school all excited. His
mom was excited that *he* was excited. "What was the lesson
about?" she asked.

"Oh, Moses and how the Israelites got away from the Egyptians," the little boy said.

Being a good and creative mom, she answered, "Oh great!
Now how did that story go?"

"Well, Mom," the little boy began, "you know those Israelites
were in Egypt and the Pharaoh had them good. He wasn't being
such a nice guy and all. So Moses got ticked off. And Mom, do
you remember the special robe Moses had?"

"No," his mom said, raising an eyebrow, "I don't quite remember that."

"Well, see, Moses had this special robe and inside it was
the electronic megaphone, and he took it out and said, 'Hey,

180

Israelites, let's get outa here! Egyptians, you stay there.' And they took off, and went right out into the desert until they hit up against the Red Sea. They didn't know what to do, ya know? But Moses was a sharp dude so he reached back into his robe and got his walkie-talkie and called to the helicopters to bring down the pontoons. . . ."

"Pontoons?" his mom repeated.

"Right, and they built this pontoon bridge, see. And then Moses got out his megaphone and said, 'Hey, Israelites over here, and you Egyptians'—the Egyptians had snuck up behind—'you ol' Egyptians, you stay right there.' And when the Israelites got to the other side, Moses reached back into his robe, got his walkie-talkie, called to the jet planes, and they came down and bombed the pontoon bridge just before the ol' Egyptians got there." The little boy caught his breath, and then said, "That's how the Israelites got away."

His mom, as you might imagine, was a little dumbfounded. She said, "Now, is that *exactly* the way the teacher told you the story?"

The little boy looked somewhat sheepish and said, "Well, Mom, not exactly—but if I told you the way she said it *you'd never have believed it!*"

Sometimes we really don't believe it the way the Bible says it. It's hard to believe that God calls us—*us*—to "re-present" him to the world. He could have done it so much better and easier in more spectacular ways. But the Bible says, "*Be my witnesses.*" It says, "*You* are the body of Christ." We are simply called to be reflections of the living Jesus Christ in the world today. We re-present him every time we meet people, and work with people. There's no getting around it.

Recent studies indicate again that the number one way to change behavior is through *modeling*. Again, *who we are is more important than what we say.*

The problem is, our models can be either good or not so good. We are witnesses, whether we want to be or not. Joe White, who runs one of the largest and finest Christian camps in America, tells a story about working with an elderly but vigorous man one day, chopping wood. After they'd almost worked a full day together and had established a relationship, Joe decided to move the conversation to spiritual things. "Sir, do you know Jesus Christ as your personal Savior?" he asked the man.

"No, and I don't want to, either," said the man with such strength and force that Joe was taken aback.

"You feel very strongly about this, don't you?" Joe asked.

"Yes, I do," the man answered.

"Do you mind if I ask why?" Joe said.

"Twenty-five years ago," the man explained, "I chopped some wood for a church nearby here and worked real hard for them. They never paid me. I felt like if that is what Jesus' followers are like, then I don't want to get to know what Jesus is like."

We re-present Christ everyday in every action of our lives— good or not so good. The servant leader knows this and lives accordingly.

5. *A servant leader looks for and fills the gaps wherever he/she is.*

There are "gaps" all around us, like the one in the book of Ezekiel. They are in our homes, in our workplace, in our daily world.

Mother Teresa, obviously one of the greatest servant leaders alive, keeps reminding those who ask that the greatest call of servant leadership is in our own homes. We don't need to go around the world; we don't need to move to Calcutta. Servant leadership is a lifestyle, wherever our lives are.

So, we should simply begin recognizing the gaps around us, and compassionately, competently respond to them. What servant leaders try to do more than anything else, by our being and doing, is bring God into those situations. Maybe the home is the hardest place to do this very vital thing, but it is where it is most needed. How can we serve others beyond our doors if we first don't practice this lifestyle at home, where real life goes on? Our servant leadership starts there, and then spreads to our neighborhood, our schools, our church, our work, and to the world.

6. *A servant leader is a creative problem-solver.*

Tom Sine makes a vital point over and over: Living in the twentieth century, above all else, means living creatively. Most of us assume that the future is going to be the same as today. We plan as though the future is simply going to be more of the present. But of course, it isn't. One reason it's called the future is because it's the future. We have only clues as to what it will be like.

So, the servant leader must live creatively, always ready to try new things, to attempt new ways to serve. Sometimes that takes looking at a problem from a whole new angle. We spoke earlier of Buckminster Fuller's book, *Synergetics*. His idea, if you remember, is that one plus one could equal more than two, because combined effort sometimes exceeds the sum of its parts. Such thinking is creative, problem-solving thinking. It's looking at seemingly two-dimensional problems in three-dimensional ways. There is a solution to most needs, if we are creative enough to see it. And the servant leader can nurture a sense of solving problems in unusual, unorthodox, and sometimes even outlandishly simple ways.

A certainly unorthodox instance that illustrates this kind of uncommon creativity is given us in a story by Alexander Calandra (source unknown):

> Sometime ago, I received a call from a colleague who asked if I would be the referee on the grading of an examination question. He was about to give a student a zero for his answer to a physics question, while the student claimed he should receive a perfect score and would if the system were not set up against the student. The instructor and the student agreed to submit this to an impartial arbiter, and I was selected.
>
> I went to my colleague's office and read the examination question: "Show how it is possible to determine the height of a tall building with the aid of a barometer."
>
> The student had answered: "Take the barometer to the

top of the building, attach a long rope to it, lower the barometer to the street, and then bring it up, measuring the length of the rope. The length of the rope is the height of the building."

I pointed out that the student really had a strong case for full credit, since he had answered the question completely and correctly. On the other hand, if full credit were given, it could well contribute to a high grade for the student in his physics class. A high grade is supposed to certify competence in physics, but the answer did not confirm this. I suggested that the student have another try at answering the question. I was not surprised that my colleague agreed, but I was surprised that the student did.

I gave the student six minutes to answer the question, with the warning that his answer should show some knowledge of physics. At the end of five minutes, he had not written anything. I asked if he wished to give up, but he said no. He had many answers to this problem; he was just thinking of the best one. I excused myself for interrupting and asked him to please go on. In the next minute, he dashed off his answer which read:

"Take the barometer to the top of the building and lean over the edge of the roof. Drop the barometer, timing its fall with a stopwatch. Then, using the formula $S = 1/2\ at^2$, calculate the height of the building."

At this point, I asked my colleague if he would give up. He conceded, and gave the student almost full credit.

In leaving my colleague's office, I recalled that the student had said he had other answers to the problem, so I asked him what they were.

"Oh yes," said the student, "there are many ways of getting the height of a tall building with the aid of a barometer. For example, you could take the barometer out on a sunny day and measure the height of the barometer, the length of its shadow, and the length of the shadow of the building, and by the use of a simple proportion, determine the height of the building."

"Fine," I said. "And others?"

"Yes," said the student. "There is a very basic measurement method that you will like. In this method, you take the barometer and begin to walk up the stairs. As you climb the stairs, you mark off the length of the barometer along the wall. You then count the number of marks and this will give you the height of the building in barometer units. A very direct method.

"Of course, if you want a more sophisticated method, you can tie the barometer to the end of a string, swing it as a pendulum, and determine the value of 'g' at the street level and at the top of the building. From the difference between the two values of 'g,' the height of the building can, in principle, be calculated.

"Finally," he concluded, "there are many other ways of solving the problem. Probably the best is to take the barometer to the basement and knock on the superintendent's door. When the superintendent answers, you speak to him as follows: 'Mr. Superintendent, here I have a fine barometer. If you will tell me the height of this building, I will give you this barometer.'"

At this point, I asked the student if he really did not know the conventional answer to this question. He admitted that he did, but said that he was fed up with high school and college instructors trying to teach him how to think . . . and to explore the deep inner logic of the subject in a pedantic way, as is often done in the new mathematics, rather than teaching him the structure of the subject.

We need to be creative, unorthodox, unintimidated by problems. And we need to learn to think in new ways. I don't think it will come as a shock if I say that we as Christians have often become insulated and ingrown in our ideas and our thinking. We need to be stretched.

7. *A servant leader will be unself-consciously involved in the world's needs.*

A friend said to me once that the problem with Scripture is not what he didn't understand, but what he did understand. Some of Jesus' concepts are hard to understand. But the problem with others is that they are not. Often, throughout this book, we've mentioned the oxymorons of Scripture, the paradoxes. One of these is that the greatest shall be the least, and the least the greatest in the kingdom. I don't think Jesus is categorically against success, but the phrase "the last shall be first" causes us to look at success in a radically different way than the world appears to see it. Jesus' idea of greatness is diametrically opposed to the ideas that daily bombard us. To be unselfconscious is almost an impossibility today. How could anyone be involved in anything without focusing on his own good deed?

Do you remember the story about my mature, Christian friend who had been radically changed by a new reading of Romans? Now that she knew she was a sinner, she explained, she finally understood that any good thing she did came from the Father. Well, that's what humility is. And that's the key to being unself-conscious. Humility is simply recognizing that what is happening when we give is coming *through* us not *from* us.

I heard a man once described as being so humble, he was reckless. In this context, that description makes very good sense, doesn't it? Humility, especially for the servant leader, is not thinking any less of yourself nor is it thinking any more of yourself. It's simply not thinking about yourself at all—being unself-consciously involved in what God is doing—through you and others—in the world. J. I. Packer, the noted author of *Knowing God*, once received what I believe is the epitome of compliments. Someone said in describing his teaching, "He was so focused, so unself-consciously involved, so immersed in what he was doing—that *he didn't even know he was there!*"

This reminds me of a conversation I had with an older gentleman. He radiated a special presence, a strong and genuine serenity. Somewhere in the midst of the conversation I remember him saying, "As I get older, I seem to place less importance on material things. . . ." Then he added, "and come to think of it, *less importance on importance.*" On my way home that night, I pondered over the question of what really is important. The more I thought about it, the more I came to recognize the wisdom of that saintly, simple man. In our overemphasis on "importance" and "appearance," we often confuse form with essence.

Servant leaders should, on occasion, ask themselves such questions as the following:
- *Does your reputation exceed your character?*
- *Which would you rather have—a Christian reputation or Jesus Christ?*
- *Have you ever loved Jesus more than you love him now?*

My wife's favorite verse begins, "Remember your first love. . . ." Many of us remember when we first became Christians, how passionate, excited, and so in love we were with the Lord. Sometimes that feeling slowly fades into dullness and routine until we get to a phase of life in which we are simply protecting our Christian reputation. It is my hope that as we grow in our relationship with God we will love him more and more each year, allowing our passion to grow. Passion is a word we Christians do not use nearly enough.

A. W. Tozer says that people who are crucified with Christ have three distinct marks:
(1) they are facing only one direction,
(2) they can never turn back, and
(3) they no longer have plans of their own.

That's not only passionate commitment, but also unself-conscious freedom in Christ. The Phillips version of Ephesians 3:14–21, mentioned in the beginning of this book, wonderfully summarizes this reality:

As I think of this great plan I fall on my knees before the Father . . . and I pray that out of the glorious riches

187

of his resources he will enable you to know the strength of the Spirit's inner reinforcement—that Christ may actually live in your hearts by your faith. And I pray that you, rooted and founded in love yourselves, may be able to grasp (with all Christians) how wide and deep and high is the love of Christ—and to know for yourselves that love so far above our understanding. So will you be filled through all your being with God himself!

Now to him who by his power within us is able to do infinitely more than we ever dare to ask or imagine—to him be glory in the Church and in Christ Jesus for ever and ever, amen!

What a prayer! God can do incredible things in ordinary people's lives, when we turn loose in Christ, when we "let" Christ work through us. As Jim Elliot so brilliantly remarked, "He is no fool who gives away what he cannot keep, in order to gain that which he cannot lose."

Is a servant leader called to be successful, or to be faithful?

Clarence Jordan was a man of unusual abilities and commitment. He had two Ph.D.s, one in agriculture and one in Greek and Hebrew. So gifted was he, he could have chosen to do anything he wanted. He chose to serve the poor. In the 1940s, he founded a farm in Americus, Georgia, and called it Koinonia Farm. It was a community for poor whites and poor blacks. As you might guess, such an idea did not go over well in the Deep South of the '40s.

Ironically, much of the resistance came from good church people who followed the laws of segregation as much as the other folk in town. The town people tried everything to stop Clarence. They tried boycotting him, and slashing workers' tires when they came to town. Over and over, for fourteen years, they tried to stop him.

Finally, in 1954, the Ku Klux Klan had enough of Clarence Jordan, so they decided to get rid of him once and for all. They came one night with guns and torches and set fire to every building on Koinonia Farm but Clarence's home, which they riddled with bullets. And they chased off all the families except one black family which refused to leave.

Clarence recognized the voices of many of the Klansmen, and, as you might guess, some of them were church people. Another was the local newspaper's reporter. The next day, the reporter came out to see what remained of the farm. The rubble still smoldered and the land was scorched, but he found Clarence in the field, hoeing and planting.

"I heard the awful news," he called to Clarence, "and I came out to do a story on the tragedy of your farm closing."

Clarence just kept on hoeing and planting. The reporter kept prodding, kept poking, trying to get a rise from this quietly determined man who seemed to be planting instead of packing his bags. So, finally, the reporter said in a haughty voice, "Well, Dr. Jordan, you got two of them Ph.D.s and you've put fourteen years into this farm, and there's nothing left of it at all. Just how successful do you think you've been?"

Clarence stopped hoeing, turned toward the reporter with his penetrating blue eyes, and said quietly but firmly, "*About as successful as the cross.* Sir, I don't think you understand us. What we are about is not success but faithfulness. We're staying. Good day." Beginning that day, Clarence and his companions rebuilt Koinonia and the farm is going strong today.

Clarence understood servant leadership. The essence of the lifestyle we are seeking is not necessarily success, but faithfulness. The success of our servant leadership is measured in our faithfulness to our calling.

And what is that calling? To be our best, to discover and utilize the magnificent potential within us, and then to give it all away in a lifestyle of servant leadership. Servanthood must become a part of our nature through the continual work of the cross in our lives. In the ultimate weakness of Christ's cross, infinite power was set loose in the world.

Doug McGlashan is a living example of what this book is hoping to be about. His servant's heart is enhanced by superb leadership skills. He recently showed me something he had written for *World Vision* magazine, "The Towel." Since "the end is where we start from" I believe it offers us an appropriate and challenging final thought:

The Towel

Still wet, grimy from eleven pairs of feet, a towel hangs in a corner alongside a wash basin. As usual.

Tonight, though, is different. The towel was not hung there by the servant girl, but by the one they call Master, Teacher. The Master doing a servant's work for his followers? That's all wrong. Somehow, though, he makes it right.

For a few moments eleven pairs of eyes fix thoughtfully on the towel and basin. But tonight of all nights there are more pressing matters.

Wait! Is he saying wash one another's feet? What if this little band takes him seriously? What if they actually imitate their self-appointed foot-washer? Tomorrow, of course, morning-after realism will unmask the thought for the nonsense it is.

But tonight, in the glow of the moment, imagination rules. *Could a servant's towel be the rumpled banner of a new way? Not likely, people being what they are. But maybe. Just maybe.*

"Now to him who
   by his power within us
   is able to do infinitely more
   than we ever dare to ask or imagine
to him be the glory in the Church and in Christ Jesus
for ever and ever, amen."

Amen.

Great Lady

Epilogue

Throughout the book I have tried to emphasize that peak performers come in all shapes, sizes, and ages. The following is a short tribute to one of the greatest peak performers I've known in my lifetime. If ever a person could be described as having "a passion to be the best—and being willing to give it all away" it is this one.

I remember when I was in the fourth grade and you used to do things like stay up half the night just to make me a Zorro outfit for Halloween. I knew you were a good mom, but I didn't realize what a great lady you were.

I can remember your working two jobs sometimes and running the beauty shop in the front of our home so as to insure that our family would be able to make ends meet. You worked long, long hours and somehow managed to smile all the way through it. I knew you were a hard worker, but I didn't realize what a great lady you were.

I remember the night that I came to you late . . . in fact, it was near midnight or perhaps beyond, and told you that I was supposed to be a king in a play at school the next day. Somehow you rose to the occasion and created a king's purple robe with ermine on it (made of cotton and black markers). After all that work I still forgot to turn around in the play, so that no one really saw the completion of all your work. Still, you were able to laugh and love and enjoy even those kinds of moments. I knew then that you were a mother like no other who could rise to any occasion, but I didn't realize what a great lady you were.

I remember when I split my head open for the sixth time in a row and you told the school, "he will be okay. Just give him a little rest. I'll come and check on him later." They knew and I knew that you were tough, but I didn't realize what a great lady you were.

I can remember in junior high and high school you helping me muddle through my homework—you making costumes for special events at school—you attending all my games. I knew at the time that you would try almost anything, if it would help one of your children, but I didn't realize what a great lady you were.

I can remember bringing forty-three kids home at 3:30 one morning when I worked for Young Life and asking if it would be okay if they stayed over for the night and had breakfast. I remember you getting up at 4:30 to pull off this heroic feat. I knew at the time that you were a joyous and generous giver, but I didn't realize what a great lady you were.

I can remember you attending all my football and basketball games in high school and getting so excited that you hit the person in front of you with your pompons. I could even hear you rooting for me way out in the middle of the field. I knew then that you were one of the classic cheerleaders of all time, but I didn't realize what a great lady you were.

I remember the sacrifices you made so that I could go to Stanford—the extra work you took on, the care packages you sent so regularly, the mail that reminded me that I wasn't in this all alone. I knew you were a great friend, but I didn't realize what a great lady you were.

I remember graduating from Stanford, and deciding to work for two hundred dollars a month loving kids through Young Life. Although you and Dad thought I had fallen off the end of the ladder you still encouraged me. In fact, I remember when you came down to help me fix up my little one-room abode. You added your special, loving touch to what would have been very simple quarters. I realized then—and time and time again—what a creative genius you were, but I didn't realize what a great lady you were.

Time wore on, I grew older and got married, and started a family. You became "NaNa" and cherished your new role, yet you never seemed to grow older. I realized then that God had carved out a special place in life when he made you, but I didn't realize what a great, great lady you were.

I got slowed down by an accident. Things got a little tougher for me. But you stood alongside as you always had. Some things, I thought, never change—and I was deeply grateful. I realized then what I had known for a long time—what a great nurse you can be—but I didn't realize what a great, great lady you were.

I wrote some books, and people seemed to like them. You and Dad were so proud that sometimes you gave people copies of the books just to show what one of your kids had done. I realized then what a great promoter you were, but I didn't realize what a great, great lady you were.

Times have changed . . . seasons have passed, and one of the greatest men I have ever known has passed along as well. I can still remember you at the memorial service, standing tall and proud in a brilliant purple dress, reminding people, "How blessed we have been, and how thankful we are for 'a life well lived.'" In those moments I saw a woman who could stand tall and grateful amidst the most difficult of circumstances. I was beginning to discover what a great, great lady you are.

In the last year, when you have had to stand alone as never before, all of what I have observed and experienced all those years have come together in a brand new way. In spite of it all, now your laughter is richer, your strength is stronger, your love is deeper, and I am discovering in truth what a great, great lady you are.

Thanks for choosing me to be one of your sons.

tim

After the final no there comes a yes,
And on that yes
the future of the world depends.
—*Wallace Stevens*

Tim Hansel is president of Summit Expedition, a nonprofit California corporation providing adventure-based educational experiences for people of all ages and backgrounds. Tim is highly sought after as a speaker and seminar leader. For more information about Summit Expedition, or for information regarding films, books, or speaking engagements, write to:

Tim Hansel
Summit Expedition
P.O. Box 521
San Dimas, California 91773
818/915-3331

Notes

1. Major W. Ian Thomas, *The Saving Life of Christ* (Grand Rapids, Mich.: Zondervan, 1961), 64–65.

2. Frederick Buechner, *Hungering Dark* (San Francisco: Harper and Row, 1969), 13–14.

3. Martin Bell, *The Way of the Wolf* (New York: Seabury Press, 1968), 43.

4. Oswald Chambers, *My Utmost for His Highest* (New York: Dodd, Mead and Co., 1935), 151.

5. Becky Manley Pippert, *Out of the Salt Shaker* (Downer's Grove, Ill.: InterVarsity Press, 1979), 40–41.

6. Eugene Peterson, *Traveling Light* (Downer's Grove, Ill.: Inter-Varsity Press, 1982), 45.

7. Phil. 4:19; Matt. 6:25; Luke 12:32; Matt. 6:33; Prov. 23:7 KJV; Mark 9:24 KJV; James 2:17; Rom. 8:31; Matt. 7:7; Mark 11:24.

8. John Powell, *The Secret of Staying in Love* (Allen, Tex.: Argus Communications, 1974), 11.

9. "How to Stop Wasting Time—Experts' Advice," *U.S. News & World Report* 92 (Jan. 25, 1982), 51–52

10. Herb Gardner, *A Thousand Clowns* (New York: Penguin Books, 1961) 70, Act 2.

11. Alan Loy McGinnis, *Bringing Out the Best in People* (Minneapolis: Augsburg, 1985), 66–67.

12. Lois Cheney, *God Is No Fool* (Nashville: Abingdon Press, 1969), 140–141.

13. Charles W. Colson, *Loving God* (Grand Rapids, Mich: Zondervan, 1983), 25.

14. McGinnis, 76.

15. Lewis B. Smedes, *How Can It Be All Right When Everything Is All Wrong* (New York: Harper and Row, 1982), 11, 15.

16. Clyde H. Reid, *Celebrate the Temporary* (New York: Harper and Row, 1972), 43–44.

17. George Bernard Shaw, *Man and Superman, Plays by George Bernard Shaw* (New York: Signet Classics, 1960), 257.

18. Henri Nouwen, "The Desert Counsel to Flee the World," *Sojourners,* June 1980, 18.

19. John White, *The Fight* (Downer's Grove, Ill.: InterVarsity Press, 1978), 61.

20. Frederick Buechner, *Wishful Thinking* (San Francisco: Harper and Row, 1973), 85–86.

CHRISTIAN HERALD
People Making A Difference

Christian Herald is a family of dedicated, Christ-centered ministries that reaches out to deprived children in need, and to homeless men who are lost in alcoholism and drug addiction. Christian Herald also offers the finest in family and evangelical literature through its book clubs and publishes a popular, dynamic magazine for today's Christians.

Our Ministries

Family Bookshelf and **Christian Bookshelf** provide a wide selection of inspirational reading and Christian literature written by best-selling authors. All books are recommended by an Advisory Board of distinguished writers and editors.

Christian Herald magazine is contemporary, a dynamic publication that addresses the vital concerns of today's Christian. Each monthly issue contains a sharing of true personal stories written by people who have found in Christ the strength to make a difference in the world around them.

Christian Herald Children. The door of God's grace opens wide to give impoverished youngsters a breath of fresh air, away from the evils of the streets. Every summer, hundreds of youngsters are welcomed at the Christian Herald Mont Lawn Camp located in the Poconos at Bushkill, Pennsylvania. Year-round assistance is also provided, including teen programs, tutoring in reading and writing, family counseling, career guidance and college scholarship programs.

The Bowery Mission. Located in New York City, the Bowery Mission offers hope and Gospel strength to the downtrodden and homeless. Here, the men of Skid Row are fed, clothed, ministered to. Many voluntarily enter a 6-month discipleship program of spiritual guidance, nutrition therapy and Bible study.

Our Father's House. Located in rural Pennsylvania, Our Father's House is a discipleship and job training center. Alcoholics and drug addicts are given an opportunity to recover, away from the temptations of city streets.

Christian Herald ministries, founded in 1878, are supported by the voluntary contributions of individuals and by legacies and bequests. Contributions are tax deductible. Checks should be made out to Christian Herald Children, The Bowery Mission, or to Christian Herald Association.

Administrative Office: 40 Overlook Drive, Chappaqua, New York 10514
Telephone: (914) 769-9000

 Fully-accredited Member of the Evangelical Council for Financial Accountability